e Cambridge Manuals of Science and
Literature

AN HISTORICAL ACCOUNT OF
THE RISE AND DEVELOPMENT
PRESBYTERIANISM IN SCOTLAND

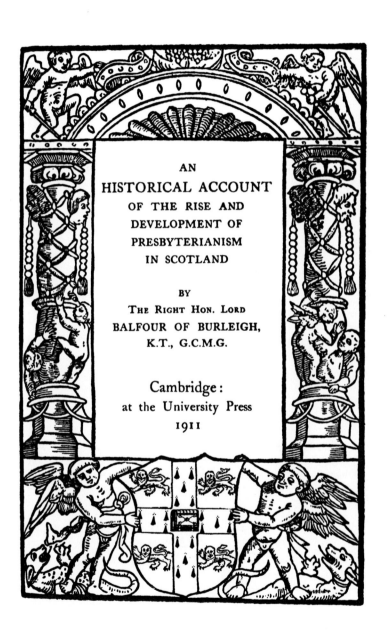

AN
HISTORICAL ACCOUNT
OF THE RISE AND
DEVELOPMENT OF
PRESBYTERIANISM
IN SCOTLAND

BY

THE RIGHT HON. LORD
BALFOUR OF BURLEIGH,
K.T., G.C.M.G.

Cambridge:
at the University Press
1911

CAMBRIDGE UNIVERSITY PRESS

Cambridge, New York, Melbourne, Madrid, Cape Town,
Singapore, São Paulo, Delhi, Tokyo, Mexico City

Cambridge University Press
The Edinburgh Building, Cambridge CB2 8RU, UK

Published in the United States of America by
Cambridge University Press, New York

www.cambridge.org
Information on this title: www.cambridge.org/9781107401938

© Cambridge University Press 1911

First published 1911
First paperback edition 2011

A catalogue record for this publication is available from the British Library

ISBN 978-1-107-40193-8 Paperback

*With the exception of the coat of arms
at the foot, the design on the title page is a
reproduction of one used by the earliest known
Cambridge printer, John Siberch, 1521*

PREFACE

THE request made to me was that I should write an historical account of the rise and development of Presbyterianism in Scotland. It was to be as full as the limitation of space would allow, and it was obviously intended primarily as much for English as for Scottish readers, and these conditions have had to be borne in mind in its preparation.

The little volume prepared in response to this request makes no pretence to original research, but only to the humbler, though perhaps not in all respects simpler, task of collecting and succinctly presenting the information made available by writers of an authority to which I cannot aspire. The limitations of space prohibit the full discussion of many controversial points, and confine me to the compilation of a fair statement founded on the agreement of the most competent authorities. It is not possible to divest oneself of Presbyterian sympathies and partiality, but an earnest effort has been made, by selection of the points which have been brought out in strongest relief, and by a fair presentation of material facts, to trace the main outlines of the whole subject in a well-proportioned and comprehensive way.

In conformity with the subject suggested to me, stress has been laid almost exclusively upon the constitutional development of Presbyterianism in

Scotland, both internally and in its relation to the State.

Throughout the whole history of the Reformed Church in Scotland one of the most outstanding features will be found to be the overwhelming desire to maintain the independence of the Church from all secular control, and the most characteristic feature of the disputes which went on during the reigns of the Stewart Kings (especially James VI and I, and Charles I), was the failure of those Monarchs to appreciate the Scottish sentiments of Patriotism, Protestantism and Freedom.

I desire to express my great obligations to the Rev. A. B. Wann, D.D., Edinburgh, without whose competent assistance the task undertaken could not have been completed within the allotted time. I have also to acknowledge the courtesy of the Rev. H. Cowan, D.D., and the Rev. John Herkless, D.D., Professors of Church History at the Universities of Aberdeen and St Andrews respectively, who read through the proofs and gave me much valuable advice. I have also to acknowledge the cordiality with which the Rev. Canon Mitchell, of Coates Hall, Edinburgh, assisted me in securing that injustice should not be done to the Scottish Episcopal Church in my narrative.

BALFOUR OF BURLEIGH.

10 *March* 1911.

CONTENTS

CHAPTER 1

SCOTLAND ON THE EVE OF THE REFORMATION

THE Scottish Church entered upon its Presbyterian phase at the Reformation. It has been contended that in doing so it was but returning to the organisation of the ancient Celtic Church. But while it is an undoubted fact that the presbyter abbots of Iona exercised authority over the Church which they founded, it seems to be also a fact that they consecrated, or caused to be consecrated, bishops for its service if not for its rule. In any case, the Celtic Church was fully Romanized in the reign of David I (1124–1153); and the Reformers, in so far as they departed from Roman usages, built not upon any relics of the ancient Celtic foundation, but, as they believed, upon the word of God. To trace from the beginning the development of Presbyterianism in Scotland it is not necessary, therefore, to go further back than the sixteenth century.

At that time Scotland was a poor and backward

country. Neither agriculture nor manufactures had been highly developed; and its minerals were scarcely touched. There was a good deal of pasture, of which the products found their way in considerable quantities to the Netherlands. Already the scantiness of the woods and forests, so noticeable until recent times, had been remarked, and had been made, but ineffectually, the subject of remedial legislation. Waste and bog covered large areas which are now smiling meadows and cornfields. Edinburgh, the capital and largest town, cannot have had more than 30,000 inhabitants; while the total population of the country may not have exceeded 500,000.

Yet the Scottish people were not, on the whole, either degraded or destitute. Their agriculture and pasture served their needs; and in general they enjoyed the fruit of their own labours. However devoted to their feudal lords they may have been, they were not mere serfs. The officers of more than one French auxiliary force were disagreeably surprised to find a peasantry who were ready and able to offer effectual resistance to high-handed dealings with their possessions. Their prowess in war was acknowledged; and their patriotism was fervent.

The Stewart dynasty, which had come to the throne through the marriage of the Steward of Scotland to the daughter of the great king and national hero, Robert the Bruce, had for two cen-

turies ruled the land, and enjoyed the full allegiance
of the people, though the turbulence and ambition of
the nobles, and the feudal loyalty which bound their
tenants to them, had kept down the regal power.
The deaths at early ages of so many kings, and the
subsequent minorities of their successors, had often
given opportunity for the rule of factions ; and the
Scottish nobility were accustomed to enter into
"Bands" or Covenants with one another for mutual
defence and sometimes mutual aggrandisement. The
Parliament never had the weight and authority of
the Parliament in England; from which, it should be
remarked, two peculiarities distinguished it. The
Lords Spiritual, the Lords Temporal, and the
Commons sat together in one House. At the beginning of each Parliament, certain members, entitled
the Lords of the Articles, were chosen to prepare the
business, with the result that a Parliament, as a rule,
did little more than register what the Lords of the
Articles had decided.

One great steadying and unifying influence did
much to preserve the often distracted land from
anarchy and disruption. King, nobles, clergy, and
people were very generally united in a common
jealousy of England ; and the attempts of the larger
country, often renewed through three centuries, to
subjugate and annex the smaller, had welded the
Scottish nation into a unity which its perpetual

faction-fights tend to obscure. Since the days of the first Edward, alliance with France against England had become the traditional policy of Scotland, and when war threatened, Scotsmen, as a rule, laid aside their feuds and cheerfully prepared for yet another struggle with their "auld enemy of England."

A large part of the country (though inhabited by a relatively smaller portion of the population) was but imperfectly united to the rest. The Highlands of Scotland, including the north-western part of the country, were peopled by a race whose language was absolutely foreign to their neighbours in the south and east; their manners and institutions were widely different, and their allegiance to the Crown was weak in comparison with their devotion to their own chiefs. Indeed, it was not until the reign of James IV (1488–1513) that the Highlands and Islands were first completely subjugated; and until after 1745 these differences made many a mark upon the political history of Britain. On the course of Scottish ecclesiastical history also they have exercised an influence, important indeed, but less obvious, for the discussion of which a work like the present does not offer sufficient scope.

Ecclesiastically, Scotland was divided into thirteen dioceses. The ancient see of St Andrews had received Archiepiscopal and Metropolitan rank in 1472; but in 1492 (old style 1491) Glasgow also had attained this honour, probably not without the intention on the part both of the King and of the Pope that, as in England York was of use in curbing the claims of Canterbury, so in Scotland Glasgow might bridle St Andrews. Under the latter remained the dioceses of Brechin, Aberdeen, Moray, Ross, the Isles, Caithness, and Orkney; under the jurisdiction of the former were put Galloway, Dunblane, Dunkeld and Lismore (Argyll). At a later period Dunblane and Dunkeld were restored to St Andrews and the Isles were handed over to Glasgow. The parishes of Scotland numbered about a thousand, and over five hundred chapels supplemented the parish churches in supplying the religious wants of the people. Some forty collegiate churches, each with its provost (dean) and chapter, were established in important centres. Over a hundred religious houses, belonging to a great variety of orders of monks, friars and nuns, were scattered over the country; and there were nearly as many hospitals for the maintenance of the aged and disabled poor.

The wealth of the Church was enormous in proportion to the resources of the country. In rents and dues of various kinds it was computed to enjoy as much as the other Estates combined. The Church land was mainly held by the religious houses; and as some seven hundred out of the thousand parishes had also been annexed to them or to the bishoprics, the greater teinds, or tithes, went to swell the revenues of the more important churchmen, leaving only a pittance for the vicars who ministered as parish priests. Thirty-two mitred abbots and priors sat as Spiritual Lords in Parliament along with the thirteen bishops. This concentration of wealth and power in the hands of the religious orders, the result of their original reputation for superior piety, self-denial and zeal, began to generate the deepest odium when sloth, luxury and vice invaded their houses, and the impoverished and disabled members of the lay community saw these great endowments squandered upon able-bodied but lazy and self-indulgent churchmen.

Education had not become general in Scotland. Yet a considerable number of schools had been founded, mainly in connection with the religious houses ; and the country boasted three Universities, all established in the preceding century. In 1413, the Pope's bull had confirmed the erection of the University of St Andrews, set on foot two years previously. Glasgow followed in 1450, and Aberdeen in 1494. In each case, the bishop of the diocese had taken the leading part in founding the new school of learning. Nor was an appreciation of the practical value of education wanting, when we find Parliament in 1496 passing an Act to compel barons and freeholders of substance to have their eldest sons and heirs educated in Latin, philosophy and law, that in

future days they might become competent sheriffs
and judges through all the realm.

During the reign of James V (1513–1542) the
country was being prepared for a religious revolution.
Scotland shared, though late, in the general intellectual awakening which characterized the age, and
which of itself tended to shake old institutions that
could not justify their existence to the minds of
keen-eyed critics.   It had also its share of earnest
souls who, whether actual Lollards or not, sighed for
the return of a purer and more primitive faith, discipline and worship than those they saw around
them.   These higher influences were reinforced by
the universal disgust of the laity at the immorality,
greed, and oppression of the clergy.   Zeal for pure
doctrine alone could not have overthrown the Roman
Church in Scotland.   It fell because its corruption
was incurable, and it had ceased to command respect
from the laity.

The literature of the time, the State Papers, the
Acts of Parliament, and the Acts of the Provincial
Councils of the clergy themselves, bear witness to
wide-spread and deep-rooted evils.   The immorality
of the clergy was notorious, and many of the bishops
were amongst the worst offenders.   Archbishop
Hamilton of St Andrews, the Primate of the Scottish
Church at the Reformation, had three natural sons
legitimated ; Cardinal Beaton, his predecessor, had

at least five. The people were glad to find a priest who would live decently and quietly with one woman; it was some security for the honour of their families. Celibacy was too frequently a name covering concubinage or debauchery. The learning of many of the clergy was on a level with their morals. They could not preach, they did not understand the Latin of their services, and when, in 1552, a belated Catechism in the vernacular was prepared and ordered to be read in church, the most stringent instructions had to be issued to the clergy to practise reading it beforehand with all zeal and assiduity lest they should stammer and stumble in their reading. The parochial clergy were blamed for their oppression of the poor. Teinds seem to have been paid without demur; these were regular burdens which were foreseen and manageable, and seemed to have warrant in Holy Writ. But the "corpse-presents" demanded on the occasion of a death, and other exactions of a like nature, were resented as shameful and oppressive extortion. The monks had no longer the character of considerate landlords; and the clergy as a body were deemed guilty of unblushing avarice. Monks and friars of no utility and doubtful morality enjoyed for themselves the rich benefactions of which they should have been but the trustees and almoners; and the beggars of the country counted them their enemies and supplanters.

Among the higher beneficed clergy, a shameful condition of affairs prevailed, for which Popes and Kings, prelates and great barons must all be held responsible. Benefices were purchased for money from King and Pope. They were conferred not only on unworthy clerics, but *in commendam* on laymen, even on children. Four of King James V's bastard sons held four of the most valuable abbeys and priories in Scotland, even from childhood, with permission of the Pope. Prelates dilapidated their benefices in favour of their illegitimate children, kinsfolk and friends, alienating lands and conferring long leases. And the nobles naturally joined in making plunder of the Church wherever they had any rights or personal influence in the disposal or management of benefices. The scramble for Church lands after the legal establishment of the Reformation in 1560 was but a continuation and acceleration of a process which had begun at least a century before.

While churchmen of high and low degree were thus falling into greater and greater disrepute with the people, the advance of enlightenment was beginning to discredit the system of faith and worship of which they were ministers. Indulgences, pilgrimages, relics, and image-worship had long furnished themes for the satirist. The impostures connected with them had created a disgust which prepared men's minds for the reception of teaching which cut

at the root of such things. The stewards of the
mysteries of God had so exercised their stewardship
that men began to question not only their fitness to
be stewards but also the value of the mysteries whose
administrators they professed to be. Things were
ripe for change.

Scotland had not been uninfluenced by the move-
ment connected with the names of Wiclif in England
and Hus in Bohemia. James Resby, an English
Presbyter, had suffered death by fire at Perth in
1407 for his anti-papal teachings; and in 1433 Paul
Craw or Crawar, a Bohemian physician, suffered at
St Andrews in like manner and for the same cause.
Laws against Lollardy and heresy continued to be
enacted; and in 1494, thirty men and women from
Ayrshire were brought before the young king
James IV and his Council, charged with Lollardy.
Some of them were personal friends of the King;
and the trial ended in his dismissing them un-
harmed.

But a new tide of "heresy" began to advance.
Luther had issued his theses against Indulgences in
1517, and had burned the papal bull of excommunication in 1520. Luther's own writings and other
books of the same kind began to come into Scotland,
and in 1525 an Act of Parliament was passed pro-
hibiting their importation. But still they came, and
from 1526, Tyndale's English New Testament came

with them, a book quite intelligible to educated
Lowland Scots. The new opinions rooted and spread
in ground already in part prepared by the older
Lollardy. And at last an example had to be made.
Patrick Hamilton, Abbot of Ferne, a young man of
noble origin, high character, and excellent education,
who had studied in Paris and Germany, and made no
secret of his Lutheran convictions, was tried by an
ecclesiastical bench, condemned, and burned in 1528.
But others arose in his place. Some were burned,
some recanted, some were compelled to flee the
country, but many of a more obscure sort remained,
and their number continually increased. The hand
of James Beaton, Archbishop of St Andrews, and
later that of his nephew David, Cardinal Beaton,
who succeeded him, was heavy upon them; and the
young king James V, who had suffered from the
treasonable ambition of the nobles, leaned upon and
supported the clergy, though he permitted and even
encouraged the merciless satires upon their vices of
his favourite, Sir David Lyndsay.

Meantime the first steps were taken in the
English Reformation by the establishment of the
Royal supremacy and separation from Rome, followed
by the destruction of relics and images and the
dissolution of the monasteries. In vain, however,
Henry VIII sought to induce his nephew James to
follow his example, and so enrich himself. Henry

had, in concert with some of its treacherous nobility, long planned the subjugation of Scotland, and James felt it the safe course to remain a faithful son of the Church, which upheld him against the nobles. His decision had the result of making the Scottish Reformation, when it did come, a very different thing from that in England. James threw himself into the arms of France, from which he had twice chosen a wife, the second being Mary of Guise; and the consequence was war with England. The nobles, loyal as well as disloyal, refused to follow him across the border, and finally, a disgraceful rout of his army at Solway Moss hastened his end. He died in 1542 at the early age of 30, leaving his kingdom to his infant daughter, Mary, born while he was on his deathbed.

James, Earl of Arran, became Regent. He was personally well inclined to the Lutheran opinions, and public opinion was so far advanced that an Act of Parliament in 1543 permitted the reading of the Scriptures in English or Scots, and preachers under the patronage of the Regent inveighed against the corruptions of the Church. A conciliatory policy on the part of Henry might have brought about a Reformation in Scotland on lines parallel to that in England. But his ruthless invasions (in which the magnificent abbeys of the Border counties were destroyed), and suspicions of his designs upon Scottish independence, made even most of the party originally in favour of an English alliance and a reforming policy resolute in withstanding him. Cardinal Beaton won over the Regent and gained the upper hand; and Scotland, for the time, was secured for France and for Rome. George Wishart, the most eminent of the reforming preachers, was burned at St Andrews in 1546, and though the Cardinal within three months was assassinated and the castle of St Andrews taken by a band of resolute men in revolt against the Government's policy, a fleet from France compelled its surrender.

The death of Henry VIII in 1547 only intensified the conflicting elements in the situation. The Protector Somerset cruelly devastated southern Scotland in his rough wooing of the child-queen on behalf of his young sovereign Edward VI, sparing neither cottage nor tower nor church nor abbey. To Henry and Somerset must be ascribed the destruction of many ecclesiastical fabrics which popular opinion in later years falsely charged upon the Scottish Reformers. Mary was sent to France in 1548 under treaty to be married to the Dauphin; and, with French aid, Scotland held her own till internal troubles in England, and finally, in 1553, the accession of Mary Tudor to the English throne, gave her peace.

The five years of Mary Tudor's reign were seemingly perilous for Protestantism in Western

Europe. England was reconciled to Rome, and the fires at Smithfield consumed such of her leading "heretics" as had not escaped to the Continent; while Mary of Guise became Regent in Scotland (1554), and strove to make it virtually a province of France. But the sovereigns of Europe set their own political aggrandisement above the common duty of extirpating heresy; and their disunion proved to be the salvation of the Reformation. Married to Philip of Spain, Mary Tudor had to join in his war against France; and Mary of Guise summoned Scotland's array for the invasion of England. But the nobles refused; they were not inclined to make their country a cat's-paw for France. Meantime the leaven of reforming teaching was continuing to work strongly among them, and even more strongly among the citizens of the towns. Companies of earnest men and women began to assemble regularly for worship and hearing sermons. They even began to form themselves into congregations under ministers who gave them the two sacraments of the reformed theology, and elders who shared with these the government of the congregation. They separated themselves from the Roman communion and worship. Their leaders at length determined to make an attempt to win open toleration, as well as to unite in one the scattered bands of Protestants throughout the kingdom. They signed, in 1557, a Covenant to maintain and establish "the most blessed Word of God and His Congregation" against all their enemies. In conformity with this Covenant they claimed that not only should quiet assemblies for preaching and teaching be allowed, but also that in the services of the parish churches the Common Prayer Book (King Edward's) and its Scripture Lessons should be used. The "Lords of the Congregation," as they came to be called, had thrown down the gauntlet; they had practically demanded the recognition of a privately organised Reformed Church, and they had urged changes in the public services which might eventually lead to the transformation of the whole from Roman to Protestant worship.

Mary of Guise herself was not a persecutor; and the Scottish Church had shown some signs of yielding to the times. The Council of Trent, then sitting at intervals, was taking measures for the internal reform of the whole Roman Church; and the Scottish clergy in their councils showed themselves awake to the same need. In 1549, they had passed sixty-eight canons which aimed at a thoroughgoing moral and administrative reform of the Church, while the tenor of these canons proves the extent and virulent nature of the corruptions prevailing. More enactments were made in 1552, and a Catechism in the Scots language was issued, in which the Roman doctrine was moderately and clearly set forth. But it was too late; the hierarchy had lost its hold of the people. Its authority was repudiated and many of its doctrines assailed by the reforming preachers, whose activity was now building up a Church organisation as well as propagating a compact and logical faith, founded upon the study of the Bible, and rejecting any merely traditional beliefs and usages.

Luther had left the supreme administration of the Church in the hands of the princes, whose power had interposed between him and the authority of the Pope ; and had merely rejected such ceremonies and usages as seemed idolatrous and sinful. The English Reformation also had been conservative in the matter of purging out ancient usages, and had to a large extent put the King in the place of the Pope. But a more thoroughgoing change had been brought in by John Calvin in the free city of Geneva. The doctrine, discipline, worship, and government of the Church there had been remodelled, as he believed, on the basis of the Word of God. And the model was widely followed. In countries such as France and Holland, where reform was resisted by the civil and ecclesiastical authorities, it was inevitable that the struggling Protestants should form themselves into communities organized without reference to existing Church laws and customs, save such as were evidently scriptural or practically expedient.

Such was the case also in Scotland. Its Church

reformers had drunk from Calvin's well. This was eminently the case with John Knox, the greatest of them all. Born most probably in 1515, of humble origin, a priest and papal notary by 1540, he had followed Wishart in 1545 and 1546, and became preacher to the garrison which held St Andrews Castle after the Cardinal's murder. Condemning their vices, but sharing their fate, he had been a French galley-slave for nearly two years. He was released at the intercession of the English Government, by whom he was employed for five years in Berwick, Newcastle, and London, forwarding the reformation under Edward VI. He was offered a bishopric, but declined to accept it. Escaping to the Continent on the accession of Mary Tudor, he finally settled for some years as minister of the English congregation at Geneva. There he worked in full accord with the great Calvin. He spent ten months in Scotland, 1555–6 ; but affairs were not yet ripe for his continuance there, and he had returned to Geneva. The Covenant of the Lords of the Congregation had been inspired by him, and the time was almost come when he was to stand forth as the leading instrument in the foundation of the Reformed Church of Scotland.

The Roman Church made a final demonstration of its power in the condemnation and martyrdom of Walter Mill, a venerable priest, in April, 1558. He

was the last who suffered death for his Protestantism.
His execution roused the Protestant lords to declare
to the Regent that they would no longer suffer their
brethren to be put to death ; and they petitioned for
liberty of worship. Their petition was granted in
part ; and they resolved to follow up their success
by asking Parliament for the suspension of the
existing laws against heresy, and a fair trial before
temporal judges for all accused of that crime. This
request not having been laid before Parliament by
the Regent, they determined to use their freedom in
setting up the reformed worship wherever they had
influence ; and the activity of the preachers redoubled.
But the tone of the Regent now changed. Her
daughter, Mary Stewart, had wedded the Dauphin in
April, and had secured for him the crown matrimonial
of Scotland.   French soldiers garrisoned the principal
fortresses in Scotland, and many offices of State were
in the hands of Frenchmen. In November, Mary
Tudor died, and the Protestant Elizabeth sat on the
English throne.   Spain, France, and the Roman
Catholics of England and Scotland looked upon Mary
Stewart as the proper successor of Mary Tudor,
Elizabeth being barred by her alleged illegitimacy and
objectionable on account of her heresy. Scotland must
be confirmed in its wavering allegiance to Romanism,
and England won by Scotland's help.

The last Council of the old Church met in March,

1559, and passed, as usual, excellent enactments for self-reformation. The Regent summoned the preachers for trial at Stirling. Joined now by John Knox, they and their supporters gathered at Perth. The Regent agreed to postpone action, but outlawed the preachers when they did not appear. Next day, May 11th, Knox thundered against idolatry in St John's Church, Perth; and on a priest's attempting to celebrate Mass thereafter, a riot broke out, the church ornaments were shattered, and a mob swept through the streets and wrecked the monasteries.

A straggling and indecisive series of conflicts and compacts ensued. The Reformers, supported by popular favour, set up their worship wherever they had power, and suppressed the religious houses. But they could not capture the fort of Leith; and failing this, their hold of Edinburgh was insecure. On the other hand, the Regent was unable to crush them in the field, or drive them from the country. A prayer for deliverance from the tyranny of the Frenchmen was inserted in the Reformed Liturgy; and application for help was made to Elizabeth. She long hesitated to aid "rebels" even privately; still longer to send them open help. But at last it became an absolute State necessity. Mary Stewart's husband had become King of France, and she Queen, in July, 1559; their designs upon England were notorious; and they had reinforced the French garrison in Scotland. An

English army joined the Lords of the Congregation in the siege of Leith ; and though they failed to take it, the garrison was so hard pressed that France consented to treat. The Regent died on the eve of the negotiations ; but the English and French Commissioners concluded a treaty (July, 1560) which virtually left Scotland free to frame her own policy. The French and the English troops departed ; and the Estates of Scotland were summoned to meet in August. The Reformation of the Church, unmentioned in the treaty, was about to receive its legal authorization.

CHAPTER II

THE REFORMATION : 1560

THE Estates met in August, 1560, and it is significant of the manner in which the Reformation was
stirring the minds of men in Scotland that the smaller
barons, exercising an ancient right, appeared unsummoned in unprecedentedly large numbers. They
were 110 out of a total attendance of 191. The
Estates requested a statement of the faith of those
who objected to the ancient order ; and in four days
there was presented to them the document known
later as the "Scots Confession," drawn up by six
ministers, Knox being one. It was remitted to the
Lords of the Articles ; and they returned it, un-
altered, for the acceptance of the Estates. It was
read through. The Primate and two other bishops
objected on the ground that they had not had time
to consider it, and five temporal lords, on the ground
that they would believe as their fathers had believed.
But by the great majority it was warmly and even

enthusiastically received, and the Estates approved
it as grounded upon the infallible Word of God.
The Reformed Faith thus received parliamentary
sanction.

A week later, the Estates abolished the jurisdiction and authority of the Bishop of Rome in Scotland,
annulled all Acts contrary to the Confession, and
made the celebration of, or attendance at, Mass
penal; the penalty for a first offence being confisca-
tion of goods, for a second, banishment, and for a
third, death. The legal establishment of the Reformed Church should have followed, but it did not.
The preachers had their scheme for the Church's
polity ready, but it contained an explicit demand
that the Teinds and the whole "Patrimony of the
Kirk" should be made available for the support of
the ministry, the schools, and the poor; and it condemned in unflattering terms the greed and oppression
of the lords and lairds who were possessing themselves unjustly and tyrannically of the Church's property and rents. The Estates were not prepared for
this "devout imagination." It involved, on the part
of many of them, restitution of what they had already
got in possession, and on the part of others, the
abandonment of designs on the ample lands and
endowments of the Church, whose ancient organisation must now crumble to pieces, leaving its patrimony
to be scrambled for. The project for the "Policy

and Discipline" of the Church was not discussed in Parliament. It came before the "Secret" or Privy Council in January, 1561, but that body declined to give it official sanction, though thirty-three of the members signed it as individuals, promising to set it forward with all their power, with the important proviso that all beneficed persons who had joined the reformers should hold their benefices for life, subject to the obligation of maintaining a ministry, according to the provisions of the Book of Discipline.

The Reformed Church, however, had vitality of its own, and was prepared not merely to struggle for its existence, but to plant its ministry and discipline throughout the land. The Congregation had already appointed eight of its leading preachers to eight of the leading towns, and five "superintendents" for the "planting of Kirks" in various districts. And in December, 1560, the first General Assembly of the Kirk of Scotland met at Edinburgh, constituted of six ministers and thirty-five laymen as "ministers and commissioners of the particular Kirks of Scotland." It proceeded to legislate for the internal affairs of the Church, and petitioned Parliament in regard to various matters. Among other things, it appointed thirty-five ministers and eight readers. It met again in May, 1561, and thereafter met regularly twice a year for consultation, administration and legislation, and to formulate the opinions and desires of the Church in matters affecting the Church, which would come under the consideration of Parliament.

What, then, was this Reformed Church in respect of doctrine, worship, government and discipline? The answer is found in the three documents known as *The Scots Confession, The Book of Common Order* (or, popularly, *Knox's Liturgy*), and the (*First*) *Book of Discipline.*

The Scots Confession.

Although the Confession of Faith was produced in four days after it was demanded, we need not suppose that it was hastily drafted. "Long have we thirsted, dear Brethren," the Preface begins, "to have notified to the world the sum of that doctrine which we profess"; and no doubt Knox and his coadjutors had already drafted the whole or at least the greater part of the Confession. It has a personal and human note running through it, and bears abundant marks of the time of controversy and struggle during which it was prepared. Following, in the main, the order of the Apostles' Creed, it set forth the doctrine of the ancient Councils, and the teachings of the Reformers on salvation, the Word of God and the work of the Spirit. It is not severely "Calvinistic," but it is strongly anti-Roman. The Catholic Kirk is defined as "a company and multitude of men chosen of God, who rightly worship and embrace him by true faith in Christ Jesus, who is the only head of the same Kirk...which Kirk is Catholic, that is to say, universal, because it contains the elect of all ages." The notes of the true Kirk of God are the true preaching of the Word of God, the right administration of the Sacraments, and ecclesiastical discipline uprightly ministered. Certain notes claimed by "the horrible harlot, the Kirk malignant" are repudiated, including "lineal descence" (in the Latin version, *successio perpetua episcoporum*). The Word of God is the ground of all teaching, and the Holy Ghost is its interpreter. Its authority is of God, and depends neither on men nor angels; "the true Kirk always hears and obeys the voice of her own Spouse and Pastor, but takes not upon her to be mistress over the same." Transubstantiation is condemned, but so is the affirmation that the Sacraments are nothing else but naked and bare figures. By Baptism we are ingrafted in Christ Jesus; and in the Supper, rightly used, Christ Jesus is so joined with us that He becomes very nourishment and food of our souls. The Sacraments are to be ministered only by lawful preaching Ministers, chosen by some Kirk, and in such elements and such manner as God has appointed. The Ministers of the Papistical Kirk are not Ministers of Christ, and have adulterated the Sacraments; their doctrine of the sacrifice of the Mass is blasphemous. The authority of the Civil Magistrate is highly exalted; and to him "chiefly and most principally the conservation and purgation of the religion appertains," including the maintenance of the true religion, and the suppressing of idolatry and superstition whatsoever.

The Confession does not touch the question of Church order except in its article on General Councils, for the assembling of which one cause is said to have been "good policy and order to be constituted and observed in the Kirk, in which, as in the House of God, it becomes all things to be done decently and in order." Then follows a significant comment:

"Not that we think that one policy, and one order in ceremonies can be appointed for all ages, times and places; for as ceremonies, such as men have devised, are but temporal, so may and ought they to be changed, when they rather foster superstition than that they edify the Kirk using the same."

In the Preface occurs the well-known acknowledgment of possible error:

"Protesting that if any man will note in this our Confession any article repugnant to God's Holy Word, that it would please him of his gentleness and for Christian charity's sake to admonish us of the same in writing; and we of our honour and fidelity by God's grace do promise unto him satisfaction from the mouth of God, that is, from His Holy Scriptures, or else reformation of that which he shall prove to be amiss."

The Book of Common Order.

No more common misapprehension in ecclesiastical matters exists than that Scottish Presbyterianism
from the beginning dispensed with a liturgy.   One of
the first tasks in every Reformed Church was the
drawing up of an order for common prayer.   That
public worship should be at the mercy of the individual who presided was never conceived or conceiv-
able by the Reformers.   An orderly form of worship
in the vernacular, which would take the place of the
Latin of the Roman service (unintelligible to the
great majority of the people), and which could be
used even where a preaching minister was not available, was manifestly a first requirement.   This was
the case, above all, in the early days of the Reformation in Scotland.   The Bible was widely read; the
readers began to draw together; under the pro-
tection of a neighbouring baron or the magistrates
of the town they gathered into a congregation.   Their
preachers were few; but there were among them
men of education, including some clerics, who could
devoutly and intelligently read the Scriptures and
prayers in public; and King Edward's (Second)
Liturgy came to have a wide and authorised use
among them.   This, however, was superseded by the

Book of Common Order, which was practically the liturgy prepared by John Knox for the use of his English congregation at Geneva from 1555 to 1559; but there were some necessary modifications and additions.

The prayers in this Book were partly drawn from the prayers of the old Church service, and partly from newer matter which from many sources had come into the common stock of all the Reformed Churches. There was also much that was peculiar to itself. Confession of sin, thanksgiving, and intercession were very prominent, and prayers for special occasions were also prescribed. There were no responses; the congregation's audible part in worship was the singing of the metrical psalms. A place for "conceived" or free prayer was expressly left before the sermon, and even the other prayers might be used as guides rather than as absolutely fixed forms. The Creed and the Lord's Prayer, doxologies and benedictions found a place.

Forms for the Sacraments were also prescribed, and for Marriage; and later on were added forms for Excommunication, Public Repentance, Visitation of the Sick, etc.

Scripture lessons were also read. And the whole formed a very full and orderly service. The Book of Common Order continued in use until the attempt to force Laud's Liturgy upon the Scottish people led to a recoil in sympathy with the Puritan aversion to read prayers altogether. A certain freedom in usage was permitted to and taken by ministers who were so inclined. But the evidence seems to show that for the first eighty years of the Reformed Church, John Knox's Liturgy furnished both the matter and the form of public worship in Scotland.

The (First) Book of Discipline.

The Book of Discipline, as already mentioned, was never approved by the Estates ; and, as it dealt with much more than the purely internal affairs of the Church, could not, without that approval, become in its entirety the law of the Church. Nevertheless, the Church acted upon it as far as possible ; and, taken as a whole, it is a manifesto of the ideals and an embodiment of the spirit of the Reformers of the highest importance to any student of the development of the Church of Scotland. The Confession of Faith was never impugned ; and until the days of Charles and Laud the Scottish Church enjoyed its own Liturgy in peace, though some emendations were urged by King James after his accession to the throne of England. But the early years of the Reformed Church were full of a strenuous attempt to carry out the ideals of the Book of Discipline in the face of a semi-civilised community, an unruly baronage, and an unsympathetic Government. An outline of its chief provisions will therefore be given. The division into these chapters, it may be noted, is not in the original, which gives larger "heads."

Chapter 1. *Of Doctrine.* The Word of God is to be truly and openly preached in every church; contrary doctrines, including all obligations laid on the consciences of men without express commandment of God's Word, are to be utterly repressed. This condemns the vows, festivals, etc., of the Roman Church.

Chapter 2. *Of the Sacraments.* Baptism and the Lord's Supper are to be observed as near their original simplicity as possible.

Chapter 3. *Of Abolishing Idolatry.* The Mass, Invocation of Saints, Adoration of Images, and all honouring of God not contained in His Holy Word are to be suppressed, with all monuments and places of the same, except parish churches and schools.

Chapter 4. *Of Ministers and their lawful Election.* "In a Church reformed, or tending to reformation, none ought to presume either to preach, or yet to minister the Sacraments, till that orderly they be called to the same. Ordinary Vocation consisteth in Election, Examination, and Admission." Each separate congregation has a right to elect its own minister, failing which "the Church of the Superintendent with his Council" may present one. He is then to be examined in life and manners,

doctrine and knowledge, and in his power to preach.
He is thereafter to be admitted on "the public
approbation of the people, and the declaration of the
chief minister, that the person there presented is
appointed to serve the Church." "Other ceremony...
we cannot approve; for albeit the Apostles used imposition of hands, yet seeing the miracle is ceased,
the using of the ceremony we judge not necessary."
Even in the present dearth of ministers, "strict and
sharp" examination is necessary. It is better for
a congregation to have no minister than one unfit
and unable to preach the Gospel. But men who
have the necessary gifts should be compelled to use
them, and settled in the chief towns and through the
provinces. To churches which cannot be supplied at
present with ministers, "readers" may be appointed
to read the Common Prayers and the Scriptures; and
these, if they acquire the power of edifying preaching, may ultimately be advanced to be ministers.

Chapter 5. *Of Provision for the Ministers.*
Suitable stipends in kind and in money are suggested for ordinary Ministers, for Superintendents,
for Readers, and for Exhorters (i.e. Readers of experience who have made some progress in the power
of exhorting the people, as a step towards the
ministry). The poor and the teachers of the youth
also are to be provided for from the Patrimony of
the Kirk.

Chapter 6. *Of the Superintendents.* The reason for making a "difference between preachers at this time" is the want of ministers and the need of providing for the whole country. "And therefore we have thought it a thing most expedient at this time, that from the whole body of godly and learned men, now presently in this realm, be selected ten or twelve (for in so many provinces we have divided the whole) to whom charge and commandment should be given to plant and erect Kirks, to set, order, and appoint ministers, as the former order prescribes, to the countries which shall be appointed to their care, where none now are." The bounds of their "dioceses" are stated and their duties defined. They are not to remain over three or four months at their principal town, but to employ themselves in visitation of their dioceses, preaching at least thrice every week, and examining the life, diligence and behaviour of the ministers, the order of their Kirks, and the manners of the people. "They must further consider how the poor be provided, how the youth be instructed." Superintendents should be appointed by the Privy Council, in consultation with the principal ministers and laymen of the diocese, thereafter they are to be examined and admitted. They are to be subject to the censure and correction of the ministers and elders of their dioceses, and corrected or deposed for the same crimes as any other minister.

Chapter 7. *Of Schools and Universities.* Every Kirk should have a schoolmaster, who in rural parishes may be the reader or the minister, and shall give elementary instruction, particularly in the Catechism (Calvin's); in smaller towns Grammar and the Latin tongue are to be taught, in larger towns, colleges, in which at least Logic and Rhetoric and the tongues are taught, should be erected. Provision should be made for poor scholars; and apt scholars, both of rich and of poor parents, should be compelled to continue their education as far as possible. An elaborate scheme for the reorganization of the Universities (St Andrews, Glasgow and Aberdeen) is given.

Chapter 8. *Of the Rents and Patrimony of the Kirk.* The Kirk should be restored to her right and liberty, and unjust assignments of the teinds cancelled. The poor are to be considered, and relieved from exactions. The teinds are to be lifted for sustentation of the ministers, the schools, and the poor; the rents of religious houses, etc., are to be retained for the use of the Kirk or Kirks in the towns and parishes where they were endowed; the temporalities of Bishoprics and Cathedral Kirks are to be assigned for the upholding of the Universities and the sustentation of the Superintendents. Deacons appointed annually are to receive and administer the revenues of each Kirk, subject to audit and report to Superintendents and "the great Council of the Kirk."

Chapter 9. *Of Ecclesiastical Discipline.* That this absolutely necessary duty may be discharged effectively, rules are laid down for proceeding, slowly and gravely, against ordinary breakers of the moral law, culminating in the public excommunication "from God and from all society of the Kirk" of the obstinately impenitent, and of those guilty of great crimes. Order for public restoration of the penitent is also prescribed. "To discipline must all the Estates within this realm be subject, as well the rulers as they that are ruled ; yea, and the preachers themselves, as well as the poorest within the Kirk."

Chapter 10. *Of Elders and Deacons.* Elders and deacons are to be elected annually by each congregation (or by adjacent congregations conjoined) from a nominated list of "men of best knowledge in God's Word and cleanest life, men faithful and of most honest conversation." Elders are "to assist the ministers in all public affairs of the Kirk," and especially to watch over the morals of the people, including the minister. Ministers may be suspended, or deposed temporarily or absolutely according to their offences ; the Superintendent and his Kirk are to be appealed to in this matter. A minister must not haunt the court, nor may he be a member of the (Privy) Council. Deacons are "to receive the rents and gather the alms of the Kirk, to keep and distribute the same."

Chapter 11. *Of the Policy of the Kirk.* General directions are laid down for the Sunday and week-day services, and for the administration of the Sacraments; it is recommended that the Lord's Table be observed every quarter, avoiding the papist festivals. The public reading and interpretation of the Scriptures are commended; both reading and preaching should be in order, without "skipping and divagation from place to place of Scripture." Family instruction, singing of psalms, and prayers are laid down as a duty.

Chapter 12. *Of Prophesying, or Interpreting of the Scriptures.* In every chief town there must be a regular weekly gathering for the systematic study of the mind of the Spirit in God's Word, and to ascertain the graces, gifts, and utterances of every man. The ministers and better qualified readers of the rural parishes within six miles are also to attend this "exercise."

Chapter 13. *Of Marriage.* Rules for permission, proclamation, and celebration of marriage are laid down. Adultery is made the sole ground for dissolution of marriage. The civil power is called upon to punish sharply offences against chastity.

Chapter 14. *Of Burial.* The dead are to be buried without singing or reading (of prayers), to avoid superstition. Even sermons at funerals are deprecated. Churches are not to be made places of burial, which ought to be in open cemeteries, walled and fenced about.

Chapter 15. *Of Reparation of the Kirks.* Kirks must be with expedition repaired in the fabric and "with such preparation within as appertaineth as well to the Majesty of the Word of God as unto the ease and commodity of the people."

Chapter 16. *Of Punishment of Profaners of the Sacrament and Contemners of the Word of God.* This condemns both the idolatry of the "shaven sort, the Beast's marked-men," and the impiety of those who, without vocation, pretend to minister the Sacraments in open assembly, or, even more wickedly, in houses, without reverence, without Word preached, and without minister. The Council is called upon to make strict laws against both. (It is admitted that there is extraordinary vocation "when God by Himself and by His only power, raiseth up to the ministry such as best pleaseth His wisdom.")

The Conclusion. A final appeal is made for the Liberty of the Kirk as against its oppressors, even though they may be the "carnal friends" of the Council.

CHAPTER III

THE REFORMATION ACCOMPLISHED AND CONSOLIDATED: 1560—1572

THE aim, spirit and method of the leaders of the Reformed Church are clearly revealed in the Book of Discipline and illustrated in the struggles of the years following the ecclesiastical revolution of 1560. The thousand parishes of Scotland were to be occupied by preaching ministers, devoted to the instruction of the people, associated with lay elders and deacons and supported by the teinds. Compulsory and universal education, on a religious basis, was to train up an instructed and moral people ; and rigorous and impartial discipline was to make sharp correction of open immorality. The Roman worship was to be absolutely suppressed with all its monuments, as idolatrous. But the parish churches and buildings used or usable as schools were to be maintained in proper repair and order.

The ruling principle of the Scottish Reformation was the necessity of adherence to the Word of God in worship, life and laws, and the obligation which was held to rest upon both the ecclesiastical and the civil power of enforcing this. This principle was interpreted narrowly, as actually forbidding anything in the polity of the Church not expressly commanded in the Scriptures. Hence the abolition of the Christian festivals (in which the Scottish Church went beyond all other Reformed Churches) and the general repudiation of much that might have been considered indifferent. The corruption of the Roman Church was to the Reformers so hopeless, and the danger from it so great, that only the most sensitive scrupulosity as to superstition and idolatry could keep the Reformed Church pure.

The Reformers, in re-discovering the primary and absolute importance of the Scriptures, accepted them in a block, the Old Testament on the same level as the New, save where expressly abrogated. To this, as well as to the previous bad example of the Papal Church, must be ascribed the darker features of the following years of Scottish history, the persecution of practising Romanists as idolaters, the calling in of the sword of the civil magistrate to enforce moral and religious reformation, and the frightful proceedings against supposed witches. The stern teachings of national disaster were needed before the descen-

dants of the first Reformers learned to read the
Bible with discriminating eyes, and to assign to the
law of Moses its place as a preparation for and not
as a part of the Gospel.

To this zeal for the Word of God must mainly be
ascribed the Reformers' anxious care for the raising
up of a learned preaching ministry, and for the
instruction of the people. The mass of the population in Scotland were illiterate and superstitious;
regular and ample instruction from the pulpit and,
if possible, in the schools was necessary if they were
to be Christians in fact as well as in name, under-
standing and practising the principles set forth in
the Word of God.

However high the Reformers exalted the office
of the ministry, they did not fear the results of
educating the people; their confidence in the illu-
minating and regenerating power of the Word was
too great for that. A learned ministry opening up
and applying the Word to congregations of intelli-
gent and devout students of the same Word was
their ideal. But where the people were not yet
educated preaching was of equal need and value.
It was by preaching that the Reformed Church dis-
criminated itself from and won its victory over
Romanism in the hearts of the common people.
Their earnest exposition of and constant appeal to
the Book which their opponents owned as divine and

yet practically neglected, carried with it conviction of the righteousness of their cause.

The strictness of discipline practised was also based upon the belief that the Church could and should actually enforce the moral law which it taught from God's Word. Error there may have been in making offences out of things not really immoral, in the harshness of the sentences, and in the publicity of their execution. Time was to soften these harder features of Scottish ecclesiastical discipline. But the purity and the impartiality of the Kirk were seen in the open confession of sin and penitence required from lords and ministers of State as well as from burghers and peasants; and a lapse from virtue, which had been trivial in the Primate of the un-reformed Church, entailed, in the case of one of the original preachers of the Reformation, a public peni-tence so humiliating and terrible that in the midst of it he broke down and fled the country. The ministers did not spare their own order; and their lives were practically unchallenged. It cannot be doubted that their own fidelity to the ideal which they preached was one great cause of their success. The impartial exercise of discipline as one of the "notes" of the true Church has never ceased to mark the Scottish Church.

The freedom of the Kirk which the Reformers claimed was not merely based on theological con-

siderations as to the nature and constitution of the
Church, but was the natural issue of the history of
the previous years. The Kirk had grown to power
by the efforts of individuals voluntarily combining
in common loyalty to the Word of God under the
hostile attitude of both civil and ecclesiastical authorities; and although the State had now accepted the
Reformed doctrine, the Kirk saw that the work of
reformation and the maintenance of godliness could
only be accomplished by its retaining for itself the
responsibilities and freedom which had carried it so
far. The State indeed was a Christian State, and
had duties as such, in co-operation with the Church.
But already the Reformed Church in Scotland was
beginning to develop its characteristic view of their
relations as independent, co-ordinate and correlated
powers. No churchman was to haunt courts or to
accept civil office; the civil magistrate had his own
place divinely appointed; but so had the Church;
and in its own place it must be free.

Yet when two divinely appointed institutions are
working in the same country towards the same end,
human frailty and corruption inevitably produce
friction. The attempt to establish a line of demar-
cation between their respective jurisdictions, and
the settlement of disputes arising from alleged trans-
gressions of that line by one side or the other, form
a large part of Scottish history, both political and
ecclesiastical.

From the very beginning, the Kirk protested against two things—the laxity of the civil authorities in punishing crimes, and their cowardice and selfishness in conniving at and sharing in the seizure of the patrimony of the Kirk. To hold this and to be free to employ it for its legitimate purposes in the maintenance of the ministry, the schools, and the poor, was part of the liberty of the Kirk. But to get as large a share of it as possible for themselves was also the aim of the needy and grasping barons, the great majority of whom had cheerfully accepted the Reformed doctrine and the overthrow of the Roman hierarchy, but considered it absurd that a handful of preachers and their lay coadjutors should serve themselves heirs to the broad lands and ample teinds of the unreformed Church. By open seizure, by assignment from the Council and, later, from the Crown, or by bargain with the prelates, they rapidly continued the work which had long before been begun of alienating Church property, so that a very small remnant, and that of the teinds alone, was available for the sustenance of the Reformed ministry.

The organization of the Church demands more detailed consideration. The Church was, in practice as well as in theory, free; it had grown to what it was by internal principle, not by ordinance of the State or by a hierarchical secession from the Roman Church; and the refusal of the civil authorities to authorize the Book of Discipline left it the more free to develop

its energies and to complete its organization autono-
mously. By necessity of the case, many of its arrangements had to be provisional. A score of preachers,
with their supporters among the barons, burgh
magistrates and people, had to organize a national
Church containing a thousand parishes (reduced
ultimately by amalgamation to about nine hundred).
It is evident that a completely finished policy, ap-
plicable to a fully settled Church, could not be at
once formulated; something must be left to time and
to the teaching of experience. Compromise, if there
were difference of opinion among the authors of the
Book of Discipline, had to be made; the main duty
before the Reformers was "the planting and erecting
of Kirks" throughout the parishes of the land. It
need not surprise us, therefore, if we find in the
productions of Knox and his five colleagues unsettled
points and open questions as to the ideal of Church
government.

The most important features which have distinguished Scottish Presbyterianism are, however,
already there in 1560. There is, for example, a
complete breach with the Roman hierarchy. Not
only the Pope but his bishops are repudiated in the
strongest terms. His priests are declared to be no
ministers of Christ. The framers of the Confession
and Book of Discipline were apparently all ecclesi-
astics, probably all presbyters of the Roman Church;

yet upon their ordination as such they set no store. Election by the people, examination by the learned, and admission by the Superintendent are prescribed for all without distinction; and there is no indication that any exception was to be made for the Roman priests who should offer themselves for the ministry. Even ordination by laying on of hands was expressly set aside. It was explicitly restored twenty years later in the Second Book of Discipline, but in all probability obedience to it did not become general at once. It is undoubtedly true that the first generation of Reformed preachers had been nearly all Roman presbyters; that within a few years they began to ordain new presbyters by the laying on of hands; and that there is therefore in the Scottish Presbyterian Churches a *perpetua successio presbyterorum* from before the Reformation. But its value to the first Reformers was *nil*. Their inward call by the Spirit, their outward call by the Kirk was the main thing; if in anything their entrance into the ministry was not so formal and regular as they made that of their later colleagues, the "extraordinary vocation" by God in that crisis of His Church was held to be sufficient warrant.

The admission of the laity to a share in the Church's discipline and rule as members of its courts and councils is, of course, an outstanding mark of the Reformed Churches. The Deacons had to do mainly with the funds of the Church; but the Elders or Seniors shared with the ministers the moral and spiritual oversight of the congregation, and could sit in judgment even upon ministers. The people had the right to elect their minister, subject to examination of his character, learning and ability; and at first the casting out of offenders and the restoration of the penitent lay ultimately with them. Hence that original publicity of discipline, which has only gradually passed away.

There remain to be considered the two great marks of Presbyterian organization—the parity of its ministers, and its rule by a graduated system of Church courts.

That the Church of 1560 and the following years was Presbyterian has been denied by some writers, who claim the Superintendents as bishops under another name. And undoubtedly the Superintendent was more than an ordinary parish minister. He was not only the minister of a chief town, but had the function of planting Kirks over a whole province. Further, he was charged not only with the admission of ministers within the province, but with a certain oversight of their life and doctrine. On the other hand, he never acted singly; the other ministers and the elders were conjoined with him in various ways. He could only "note" a minister for censure by the Kirk. In brief, he held a limited power of inspection

over the Churches of his province, and a more exten-
sive executive authority for the settling of ministers
and readers in vacant charges. He himself was subject to censure and deposition like any other minister;
and the form of his admission to office was practically
the same. It may be said, therefore, that while he
did not belong to a separate order in the ministry,
he exercised some of that episcopal power which, in
a fully organized Presbyterian Church, is exercised
by its courts, and in particular by its Presbyteries.

The Superintendentship might have developed
into a limited Episcopacy; it is possible even that
some of the framers of the Book of Discipline wished
it to do so. But in any case it was not a continuation
of the "historic episcopate"; and no attempt was
ever made to graft it on to the existing hierarchy.
The first Reformers were no advocates of Presbyterianism *jure divino*; Knox had served in the
Church of England, and his sons both entered its
ministry. But nothing which savoured of "Papistry"
found favour with them; and even in setting up
officials who had some dignity and authority superior
to the ordinary ministers they sought in name as
well as in spirit to discriminate them from the
"dumb dogs," the Bishops.

The fact is, that the Superintendent was a practical necessity. The Kirks had to be planted as
speedily as possible. The harvest was great, and

widespread, and ready. But the labourers were few. Only the towns could be furnished with a complete and settled ministry at once. The country must have an itinerant ministry for the time and a settled ministry as soon as it could be provided. The institution of Superintendents was the answer to the needs of the country. No scruples as to Presbyterian parity prevented the Reformers from setting aside five of their ablest and most influential men to plant Kirks throughout the country, while but a few of the larger towns had a settled ministry of their own.

The small number of ministers also forbad as yet the establishment of the graduated system of Church courts which soon came to be the strength and mark of Presbyterianism. Indeed it was in Scotland at this time, and contemporaneously in France, that the polity which was framed in the city of Geneva came to be developed into a system adapted to a National Church. But at least the rudiments of all of these courts were there in 1560. The Kirk-Session, as it soon came to be called, was already in operation in every organized congregation—the minister and his elders, and deacons associated with them. At the other extremity was the "Great Council of the Kirk," soon to be known as the General Assembly, formed at first of all the ministers who could attend, with the lords and barons and other men of position who were active supporters of the Reformation; and later gradually organized on a representative basis of commissioners—ministers and elders—from every presbytery. The "Council of the Superintendent's Kirk" had powers which enabled it easily to be developed into a "Provincial Synod." And as the number of parish ministers increased, the "weekly Exercise" in every important town began to acquire powers which finally made it the "Presbytery," that important court whose very name is identified with the system of Church government of which it is a part. But Synod and Presbytery existed in germ only in 1560; sufficient materials for them were not available, and in the meantime the Superintendent did much of the work which afterwards fell to them.

The creed of the Reformed Church was now publicly approved, the place of that Church in supersession of the Roman Church practically recognized, and its career as the Church of Scotland begun. It set itself to cover the land with a parochial ministry and eldership, to enlighten the whole people with the preaching of the Word, to correct their morals with a rigorous discipline, and to suppress the practice of "papistical" rites. In all these tasks, but especially the last, the Church looked for the co-operation of the civil magistrates, national and municipal, according to the laws which the Estates had made. Success, however, was measured by the degree of co-operation which the local magnates and magistrates were willing to give. In many burghs, indeed, the Reformation had taken open effect even before 1560; now it was universally accepted and enforced. The middle classes in the towns were devoted to the Reformed Church, and in return the Church strengthened them, not only by the moral and intellectual effects of its teaching and discipline, but by giving them a potent voice in its courts, and especially in the General Assembly. On every important point that touched the national welfare that assembly became, through its free deliberations and public pronouncements, a true House of Commons, a genuine representation of the people. In the country districts it was otherwise. Some of the most powerful lords remained Roman Catholic, and permitted priests at least occasionally to perform their rites. Others conformed, but winked at breaches of the law. Many had been more than content to see the collapse of the papal Church, and yet had no desire to see the rise of a strong Reformed Church, whose austere discipline would curb the licence of their lives, and whose claim to the patrimony of the Kirk would conflict with their plans of self-aggrandisement. The strong feudal feeling in Scotland made the progress of the Church slow in any district where a great noble openly or privately held by the Roman Church. It was long impossible to establish a full parochial ministry everywhere, more particularly in the North of Scotland. To this day there remain glens in the Highlands into which the Reformation, as a movement, has never penetrated. Yet progress was made from the first even in the country. Some great nobles and lords, and many lairds or smaller barons, were true friends of the Reformed Church, and used their local authority and influence to settle and maintain a ministry and to make the new courts of the Church effectual for the oversight of manners.

In one respect the history of the Reformation in Scotland is comparatively free from stain. The battle had been won from Rome at the cost of little more than twenty martyr lives, though many had suffered imprisonment and exile; and the victory was untarnished by reprisals. However severe the penal laws against "papistical" worship may seem, not more than three and probably not more than two priests suffered death in the course of the next half-century. Nominal conformity on their part seems to have been the rule; and nothing more was expected.

Whether from lack of men or of means, only five Superintendents were appointed instead of the ten or twelve intended; and no later appointments were made. Instead of Superintendents, the General Assembly began to appoint commissioners or visitors annually for the planting and oversight of Kirks in particular districts.

Nothing is at first sight more astonishing than the utter collapse of the hierarchy and of organized Roman Catholicism as a whole. It can only be explained by the total alienation of the respect of the laity, and their loss of faith in its claims. No sooner had the Lords of the Congregation summoned up courage to stand forth unitedly for their faith than it became evident that the sympathy of the country was with them; and no sooner was Scotland free to speak its mind through the Estates than the Pope and his jurisdiction were almost unanimously repudiated, the Reformed faith accepted, and the Mass penalised. Such legislation might have passed a packed Convention of Estates (though the Convention of 1560 was not packed), but it could not have been acquiesced in by the mass of the people, if any general attachment to the old system had remained, or even if the clergy themselves had retained a conviction of its divine right. Things were made easy for them by the absence of any proscription. The monasteries indeed were dissolved; but the prelates and the parochial clergy were not deprived of their benefices; and with comparatively few exceptions conformed to, or at least acquiesced passively in, the new system. A considerable number of them had long had a certain sympathy with the reformers; many whose character, learning and ability were approved became preaching ministers, and many more became readers.

4—2

Four or five of the bishops seem actually to have
become Protestants, and did not merely acquiesce
in the Reformation.

Yet the resistance passively offered by recalcitrant nobles, the difficulty created by the ignorance
and superstition of the people, the want of means
consequent on the withholding of the teinds, and the
relatively scanty supply of qualified preachers made
the progress of the Reformed Church hard. Nor
were these the only difficulties. There remained the
constant danger of the overthrow of the Reformation
by the action of the head of the State herself, with
the aid of foreign powers.

Mary Stewart, Queen of Scots, had become Queen
of France in 1559; and she and her husband, Francis,
King of France, who had also received the crown
matrimonial of Scotland, were in full sympathy with
the dominant party in France who were bent on
exterminating the French Protestants, but were
meeting with a stout resistance. The sovereigns had
sanctioned the meeting of the Scottish Estates, but
declined to confirm their Acts. It was an anxious
time both in France and in Scotland; and the sudden
death of Francis in December, 1560, brought relief
to the Protestants in both countries. By the time
Mary Stewart, a widowed girl-queen of nineteen,
returned to her native land in August, 1561, the
Reformed Church was vigorously taking possession

of the land, and John Knox, no superintendent, but
a simple minister of the Kirk, was firmly established
on his "watch-tower" at Edinburgh, the centre of
Church and State, ready to note the first sign of
danger to the national religion and the national
liberty, and to give the alarm.

Mary brought back with her the Mass, and established it in the Chapel Royal at Holyrood. Knox
would have suppressed it; but the Lord James
Stewart, the Queen's (illegitimate) brother, later to
be known as the Earl of Moray and the Good Regent,
personally guarded the door of the chapel at the first
celebration, and won most of the nobles to a more
lenient policy. For herself and for those who frequented the Chapel Royal, Mary gained toleration,
but she had also to issue a proclamation threatening
death to any who should disturb the recent settlement of religion. Knox continued openly to protest
from the pulpit against the Mass and every action
of the Queen which did not accord with the doctrine,
morality, or policy of the Reformed Church. He was
too popular and too important for the general cause
to be silenced by force. And his opposition prevented
Mary from making headway in her schemes for the
restoration of Romanism, for which she never ceased
to plot and to hope.

The Romanists and the thorough-going Reformers
seemed to be at stalemate. But the latter were

really winning. In 1561 a beginning was made of providing sustentation for the ministry. The Privy Council assigned to the Crown one-third part of the benefices of the clergy, and from these "thirds" the Crown was to provide a settled allowance for the Protestant ministers. The General Assembly continued to meet twice a year, in spite of the doubt which some of the political Protestants professed to have of the lawfulness of such Assemblies unsummoned by the Prince. "Take from us the freedom of Assemblies," said Knox, "and you take from us the Evangel. Without Assemblies, how shall good order and unity in doctrine be kept?" So early was this cardinal point in Scottish Church history seen to be all-important. The nobles mostly ceased to attend, but the ministers and elders came in increasing numbers; the Assembly came more and more to represent the opinion of the country.

In 1566 Romanism seemed on the very verge of a successful attempt at overthrowing the Reformation. Mary had impulsively chosen as her husband the Anglo-Scot Henry Stewart, Lord Darnley, son of the Earl of Lennox, a Roman Catholic of the Scottish royal blood, and next heir, after Mary herself, to the throne of England. Moray and other lords who had opposed the match, and risen in arms against it, were outlawed and driven into England. The Church proclaimed a general fast, and whispers of coming changes were in the air. But the slaughter of Riccio, Mary's Italian favourite, by the jealous Darnley and certain Protestant lords, upset political combinations. Henceforth loathing her husband, she first restored her brother Moray to his honours and her own confidence, but soon flung herself, after her husband's death, into the arms of Lord Bothwell, his murderer. The whole country felt itself outraged. Mary became a prisoner in the hands of her nobles; and was forced, while imprisoned at Lochleven in 1567, to resign the throne in favour of her infant son James, and to sanction the appointment of Moray as Regent.

The policy of the more resolute lords to deprive Mary of power had been, of course, approved by the Church; and they in return pledged themselves to complete the establishment of the Church, to make more adequate provision for the ministry, and to root out all remaining monuments of superstitious worship. The year-old king, who had been baptized with Roman rites, was now, at his coronation, anointed by a conforming bishop; and the coronation sermon was preached by Knox. Henceforth a Protestant country was to be ruled by a Protestant sovereign, and the religion of the people was bound up with their loyalty.

A largely attended Convention or Parliament in December 1567 confirmed the Acts of 1560. It put the alternative of conformity or deprivation before all teachers in schools and universities. And it made some improvement on the terms of payment of the ministers' salaries from the "thirds" already mentioned. But even this resolutely Protestant Parliament did not see its way to accept the Book of Discipline, backed though it was by the personal influence of the Regent. Too many mouths were nibbling at the patrimony of the Kirk to permit of its being handed over to the General Assembly and the ministers. It is worthy of note also that it was provided by this Parliament that the ancient lay patrons should present ministers to vacant parishes, while the examination and admission lay with the Church. Most curious of all was the Act confirming the civil privileges of the Spiritual Estate. The prelates had lost their place in the national Church, but they still held their lands, and maintained their position as the first estate in Parliament: Scotland was not prepared to revolutionize its constitution. Romanist and Protestant, clerical and lay holders of the great benefices were still the Spiritual Estate.

In these seven years, however, the planting of the Kirk had progressed wonderfully; the superintendents and commissioners had not been idle. In 1567 there were 257 ministers, 151 exhorters, and 455 readers, so that in almost every parish there was some Pro-

testant worship. The original band of less than
a score of recognized preachers had been reinforced
mainly by Roman clergy who had followed the first
Reformers; of the single house of Augustinian canons
at St Andrews not fewer than twelve had entered the
ministry. The Reformed Church had become a really
national Church, and Romanism began to be identified with continental influences which threatened
alike the independence of the nation and the reform
of religion. Protestant England under Elizabeth
harboured no designs against Scottish independence.
So Scottish statesmen of a purely secular turn of
mind, who did not share the religious enthusiasm of
the preachers, sought to preserve friendship with the
country to whose crown their queen was heir; and in
the Book of Common Order was inserted a prayer
of thanksgiving for the English aid which had de-
livered the land from oppression, and of supplication
for the maintenance of amity with England. Knox,
the former Anglican royal chaplain, was the passionate advocate of the English alliance, despite his
detestation of the "Romish rags" still clinging to
the Church of England. (He was even twitted with
his English accent, so naturally acquired!) The
march of Protestantism involved the progress of
Great Britain to unity; aiming at the former the
zealous reformers promoted the latter, aiming at the
latter (under a Scottish sovereign) politicians who

were lukewarm about religion could not but countenance the former.

The year 1567 marks the beginning of a new reign, that of James VI, as well as of a new rule, that of the Regent Moray. And as the Acts of Parliament of that year had the confirmation of the crown, whereas Mary had consistently refused to confirm those of 1560, some constitutional writers fix upon 1567 as the true date of the legal establishment of the Reformation. Unfortunately for Scotland, very little seemed to be established in any way for the next few years. Mary escaped from Lochleven in 1568, and was joined by many nobles. She was a witness of the battle at Langside, where the forces of her adherents were routed, and she fled into England, where she found herself not the guest but the prisoner of Elizabeth. Moray's firm and beneficent rule was cut short by the assassin in 1570; and a confused civil war broke out between the nobles of the King's party, headed by the succeeding regents, the Earls of Lennox and of Mar, and those of the Queen's party, who wished to restore Mary. It would be a mistake to consider these as Protestant and Romanist parties. Chivalry and diplomacy drew to Mary's side some men who were stout anti-Romanists. But the Reformed Church as such steadily adhered to the Regents; and though Lennox was slain in 1571, and Mar died in 1572, the King's party grew

stronger and stronger. The massacre of St Bartho-
lomew, 24th August, 1572, served to consolidate and
reinvigorate the Protestants of Scotland, so nearly
allied to the Huguenots of France. The regency fell
to the Earl of Morton, an able and resolute man;
and with aid from England he had crushed the remnant of the Marian party by the middle of 1573.
Romanism in Scotland was finally shattered.

On 24th November, 1572, died John Knox. He
had seen the triumph of the cause to which he had
devoted his life. The spirit of Scotland was now at
one with the spirit of Knox in the great matters of
faith and freedom; the massacre at Paris had con-
solidated the Reformation in Scotland.

CHAPTER IV

PRESBYTERY AND EPISCOPACY: 1572—1638

THE year which saw the death of Knox and the appointment of Morton to the Regency had already witnessed also the introduction of bishops into the Reformed Church of Scotland, and with them the beginning of internal dissensions which were to last for 120 years. Many considerations were operating in favour of the new departure. It would bring the Church of Scotland into closer conformity with the Church of England; it would secure the maintenance of the Spiritual Estate in Parliament in a seemly way; it would enable the work of superintendence of the "particular Kirks" to be carried out more systematically; it was hoped that it would secure the considerable remains of the old episcopal revenues for Church uses, for the abbacies and priories were now becoming hopelessly secularised. An agreement between Church and State made at a Convention at Leith in January, 1572, provided, among other

arrangements, that the old dioceses should stand, at
least till the majority of the king, but that the bishops
now to be appointed should have no more authority
than the superintendents, and should, like them, be
subject spiritually to the General Assembly. The
Assembly held in August of that year consented
reluctantly to the restoration of offices which seemed
to "sound of papistry," and expressly received the
arrangement only "as an interim." Knox counselled
the Assembly by letter to be careful as to the quali-
fications of the bishops, and to require from them
an annual "account of their whole rents and intro-
missions." The dread of Romanism, and the fear of
the bishops becoming the creatures of the State, joined
with a growing conviction of the scriptural (and
therefore divine) basis of Presbyterianism, made men
uneasy. Yet the expediency of the new departure
prevailed, and the vacant sees were filled. The new
bishops were as fiercely Protestant as any; and
Scotland to-day might have had an Episcopal national
Church but for the odium which gathered round the
name and office of bishop when it was found that
the new bearers of the title were but "tulchans"—
a name given to calfskins stuffed with straw set up
to persuade the cows to yield their milk more freely.
The first appointment was to the old primatial see
of St Andrews, which had been in Morton's hands
for a year; and his nominee, John Douglas, one of

the six authors of the Confession, entered on office after a compact which gave Morton most of the benefice and left the nominal holder but a fraction. The same was done in the case of the other bishoprics by the great men who had obtained the patronage of the sees. The Church was no richer than before, and its chief ministers were the creatures of the Regent and his friends. Bishops, therefore, were no sooner introduced than a strong reaction against them commenced.

The Church had other reasons for restiveness under the grip of the State. Morton was a stout political Protestant, but an Erastian, and no favourer of the Church's liberties nor respecter of its ministers. He starved the Church, keeping only "readers" in most of the parishes. Getting the collection of the "thirds" into his hands, he pared down and kept back the ministers' stipends. He needed money for the public service and to satisfy his private avarice, and he wrung it both from the rich prelacies and from the scanty fraction of a third of the teinds which should have gone to the parish ministers.

In 1575 Andrew Melville, who had returned to his native land after ten years' study and service in France and Geneva, raised the whole question of the lawfulness of Episcopacy. Year after year it was debated. Morton could neither bribe nor overawe Melville. He himself began to be in difficulties with his political opponents and resigned the Regency in 1578. He recovered much of his power in the following year, but he had to contend with rivals in the favour of the young king, whose personal rule had nominally begun. They succeeded finally in having Morton condemned and executed in 1581.

Meantime the Church had gone on its way, declared Episcopacy unlawful in 1580, and called upon the bishops, under pain of excommunication, to demit their offices, which most of them did within the year. In April, 1581, the General Assembly finally ordered to be registered in its Acts a Book of Policy, which it had accepted in 1578, and striven unsuccessfully to persuade the State to accept also. This Book, generally known as the Second Book of Discipline, is not only the monument of the spirit of Andrew Melville, but, as will be seen, its leading principles were afterwards accepted by the State, and it thus acquired a certain authority denied to the First Book of Discipline, which embodied the ideals of Knox and his colleagues.

Chapter 1 defines the various senses of the term "Kirk of God," claims for it independent spiritual jurisdiction under Jesus Christ, its only Head and King, and a policy founded on the Word of God alone. The jurisdictions of the Kirk and the Civil Magistrate are carefully defined, and their mutual support enforced.

Chapter 2 deals generally with the rulers or ministers of the Kirk, of whom there are four permanent and ordinary sorts (see Chaps. 4, 5, 6, 8).

Chapter 3 distinguishes extraordinary vocation or calling from ordinary, which latter alone has place in Kirks established and well reformed. Ordinary calling includes (besides the inward calling of God) election by the judgment of the eldership and consent of the people, and ordination with fasting, prayer and imposition of hands.

Chapter 4 treats of Bishops, Pastors, or Ministers (which are held to be different names for the same office), whose duty is mainly to teach the Word, administer the Sacraments, pray for and bless the people, and watch over their manners ; each is to have a particular flock.

Chapter 5 treats of Doctors, whose duty is "to open up the mind of the Spirit of God in the Scriptures." "Doctors" include the teachers in all the Schools and the Universities.

Chapter 6 treats of Elders or Seniors, whose principal duty (if they are not themselves teachers of the Word) is "to hold Assemblies with the Pastors, and Doctors who are also of their number, for establishing of good order and execution of discipline."

Chapter 7 deals with Elderships or Assemblies, of which there are four sorts—of particular Kirks, of Provinces, of a whole nation, and of all Christian nations. They are to keep pure religion and good order within their bounds, and punish transgressors ; but not to handle matters pertaining to the civil jurisdiction. Their respective duties are defined.

Chapter 8 treats of Deacons, whose duty is to receive and distribute the whole ecclesiastical goods unto them for whom they are appointed.

Chapter 9, of the Patrimony of the Kirk, claims for the Kirk all that has been given to it in past times, and denounces as sacrilege the appropriation of any part of it to the particular and "profane" use of any person. The deacons are to manage it all, including the gifts of the faithful.

Chapter 10 details the duties of the Christian Magistrate, which are to assist the Kirk, keep out false teachers, punish the contumacious, see to the maintenance of the ministry, the schools, and the poor, defend the Patrimony of the Kirk, and make laws for advancement of the Kirk and its policy, without usurping the spiritual jurisdiction. (In a corrupt Kirk, the civil magistrate may place ministers and restore the true service of the Lord.)

Chapter 11 asks for the abolition of abuses remaining in the Kirk, such as:—"papistical" titles and offices; the annexation of Kirks to such offices; the place in Parliament of such abusers of the Kirk's Patrimony their enjoyment of pluralities; the continuation of the "two-thirds" to new and idle occupants of such benefices; the new bishops, who ought to have a particular flock and no lordship over their brethren, and who, if they will not submit to the jurisdiction of the Eldership, should be deposed; men uncommissioned by the Kirk acting as for the Kirk in Council or Parliament; chapters and such-like "papistical" jurisdiction; "commissars" meddling with ecclesiastical jurisdiction; holders of the "two-thirds" dilapidating their benefices.

Chapter 12 craves Reformation according to the foregoing policy, and, in particular, the placing of a minister in every parish and reasonable congregation, very small parishes to be conjoined, and very large ones to be divided; doctors to be appointed and provided for in Universities and other needful places; elderships to be set up in all principal places, and provincial assemblies arranged; General Assemblies to be free, and supreme in ecclesiastical causes; free election of office-bearers by congregations; abolition of patronages and presentation to the cure of souls; minor benefices to be presented to scholars and bursars; the Patrimony of the Kirk to be restored to the Kirk for (1) ministers, (2) other Church officers including doctors, (3) the poor and the hospitals, (4) reparation of Kirks, and other extraordinary charges —all under management of the deacons, with yearly audit; all alienations, fees, and leases to the hurt of the Kirk to be annulled, and teinds leased, if at all, to the actual labourers of the ground.

Chapter 13 points out the religious, social, and political advantages which would flow from this Reformation.

The Church of Scotland retains to this day the main features outlined in the Second Book of Discipline, e.g. the parity of ministers, the union with them of lay elders in every court of the Church, the graded system of courts, the election of the ministers by (or with the consent of) the congregation and subject to the judgment of the Presbytery, the freedom of Assemblies, the real and independent jurisdiction of the spiritual courts, the absence of its ministers from Parliament and Council. The somewhat pedantic distinction between "doctors" and "ministers" as different orders never acquired real force, though to this day the Universities have separate representation in the General Assembly. And in most of the congregations of the Church of Scotland there are no deacons, their functions being discharged by the Kirk Session; though in other Presbyterian churches which have sprung from the Church of 1581 deacons have their place as in Melville's scheme.

In one respect the Church had already in 1581 arrived at greater definiteness and more complete organization than the Second Book of Discipline provides. The "Eldership" seems to waver between the minister (or ministers) and elders of a single congregation and the association of the office-bearers of a few conjoined. It had seemed impossible to find in single rural congregations in that comparatively rude and illiterate age enough elders to make with the minister a sufficiently qualified court. But the enthusiasm of the Church for effective organization adapted existing institutions to the plan of the eldership. The "weekly exercise" in every principal town (see p. 35, Chap. 12) was converted into an Eldership or Presbytery; while individual ministers and their elders continued, as Kirk Sessions, to rule the individual congregations. In a few years the whole country was mapped out into Presbyteries, with oversight of the churches, and Kirk Sessions within their bounds, grouped into Provincial Synods (mainly on the lines of the ancient dioceses), and represented in the General Assembly by lay and clerical commissioners. It was a time of rapid crystallization. The bishops were repudiated and brought to submission; the superintendents suffered to die out; the readers also —though they lingered long; and full-fledged Presbyterianism came into being. A more generous and honourable policy ten years earlier might have permanently established a moderate Episcopacy in Scotland. After 1581 the forces working for episcopacy had to contend with a prejudice in favour of a system which had not only a claim of divine right, but was also the self-chosen working organization of a Church free and fighting for its honour, its rights, and its responsibilities.

James VI had now reached the age of 15, and was rapidly developing those notions of kingcraft and the divine right of kings which he was to leave as a legacy fatal to his own family and dangerous to the liberties of Great Britain. He was developing them, however, under the influence of favourites who sought to use him as a tool—some for their personal ends, some for the advancement of the plans for the restoration of Romanism of which Philip of Spain was the chief author and executor. He soon came into collision with the Church, whose power he sought to curb, and whose polity he early discerned to be antagonistic to kingship, as he understood it. In doctrine he claimed to be Protestant and Calvinist; and the same year, 1581, which saw Morton's death and the Assembly's registration of the Second Book of Discipline, found James reassuring and putting himself at the head of his people by signing and issuing the King's Confession (nicknamed "the Negative Confession")—a violent and comprehensive repudiation of the pope and all his ways, most acceptable to Church and people. But a scandalous "tulchan" appointment brought the civil power and the ecclesiastical courts into conflict; for Presbyteries and Synods were now in working order. The civil power had physical force and legal form on its side; the Church courts had the still-dreaded weapon of excommunication (which carried civil consequences with it), and had, on the whole, the best of the dispute, though they could not deprive the offender of his emoluments. Again, the clergy of Edinburgh got some knowledge of the Romanist plots which were on foot and denounced from the pulpit the king's councillors concerned in them. One of the ministers was expelled from the city by the king's orders. A faction of nobles, however, by the "Raid of Ruthven" obtained possession of the king's person; and the General Assembly approved their action, because they believed that only thus had the plots been frustrated. The king escaped from custody; the nobles were forgiven upon submission and confession of guilt; the Churchmen refused to apologize. Andrew Melville, summoned before the Council, vainly claimed to be tried first by his presbytery. He was condemned by the Council to imprisonment, and had to flee, with several others, to Berwick.

The king now had his opportunity against the Church; and he took it in a parliamentary way. The "Black Acts" of 1584 declared the supremacy of the king in all causes and over all persons, made all convocations unlawful except those specially licensed by the king, lodged the chief jurisdiction of the Church in the hands of the bishops, strengthened their position as one of the three Estates, to speak evil of whom was treason, and penalized all speech slandering the king or council or intermeddling with public affairs. Freedom of Assemblies, freedom of speech, freedom of spiritual jurisdiction, were all destroyed, and Episcopacy stood revealed as the ally and tool of civil and religious despotism. Minister after minister was imprisoned or had to flee. Many moderate men were willing to see some check put upon the unbridled licence of political harangue which sheltered itself under the claim of freedom in preaching; but James went too far for them. He extorted from many of the clergy submission to the Acts, which some of them signed with the significant and convenient qualification "agreeably to the Word of God." But a recoil was inevitable. A band of exiled nobles forcibly repatriated themselves, and the exiled ministers accompanied them. The power of Arran, James's favourite councillor, collapsed; and the ministers and the Church courts resumed much of their freedom. A compromise was reached, bishops being permitted to remain, but suffered to execute their office only in conjunction with the courts of the Church, and made answerable finally to the General Assembly. The Assembly was to meet once a year; and the plan and powers of the various subordinate courts were carefully defined.

It may here be noted that during this troubled period Scotland's fourth University came quietly into existence in 1583, as the "toun's college" of Edinburgh.

In 1587 James reached his majority and signalized

it in ecclesiastical matters by obtaining an Act of
Parliament annexing the temporalities of all benefices to the Crown. The lay or laicized abbots and
priors had little difficulty in retaining what they
already held; and the temporalities of the bishoprics,
which James now won for the Crown, were begged
from him by greedy courtiers. So that of the patrimony of the Kirk there soon remained but the
"spirituality"—the teinds, of which only a part was
available for the parochial clergy, because a large
share remained as before annexed to the several
bishoprics. The Church thus lost much of what had
till then been recognized as belonging to it. But
the Act made the restoration of a real prelacy diffi
cult, and was therefore not so offensive to Presbyterians as it otherwise would have been. James and
the Church were drawing nearer. The Spanish
Armada drew them nearer still; James could not
afford to coquet with Romanism then. In 1590 he
sought a Danish bride, and a simple Presbyterian
chaplain, Robert Bruce by name, married them.
Another crowned the queen; and Andrew Melville
wrote the coronation ode. The king was acting under
the advice of a wise chancellor, Lord Thirlestane, and
he became a public panegyrist of the Kirk. Finally, in
1592, Parliament passed an Act "ratifying the liberty
of the Church, recognizing a legal jurisdiction in its
courts, abrogating the Acts of 1584 in so far as they

impinged upon ecclesiastical authority in matters of
religion, and providing that presentations by patrons
should henceforward be directed, not to the bishops,
but to the Presbyteries within whose bounds the
vacant benefices lay." It, in fact, without naming the
Second Book of Discipline, gave civil authorization to
its most important principles, and established the
Church upon a Presbyterian basis. The four succeeding years, from 1592 to 1596, were longingly remembered by the Presbyterians of the next century as the
time of the triumph and purity of Presbyterianism;
and after the struggle of a hundred years was ended,
it was upon the Act of 1592 that Presbyterianism was
restored. It was a temperate Act, recognizing an
ecclesiastical system acceptable to both clergy and
people, while not flinging the royal authority at the
feet of the ministers.

Why then did the settlement, so happily effected,
break down? There were faults on both sides.
Thirlestane had died in 1595, leaving James, the shifty
and self-opinionated, to follow his own devices, and
the more extravagant of the ministers to ruin their
own cause by the abuse of their freedom in preaching
and in Church censures, including excommunication.
Even during the halcyon years from 1592 to 1596
the leniency of the king to great Catholic nobles who
were plotting, with aid from Spain, for an open
rising against the existing settlement, made him

suspected by the General Assembly, and subjected to vituperation by the less self-controlled of the ministers. A furious attack on the conduct of the king and queen, on the court and council, and on Queen Elizabeth, by a St Andrews minister, one Black or Blake, brought things to a climax. Being summoned before the Council at Edinburgh he declined its jurisdiction. His brethren supported him, and on his condemnation a riot, excited not by the ministers but by courtiers who sought their own profit in it, terrified and infuriated the king, and discredited the champions of the Church's liberty in the eyes of many moderate men. From this time James set himself deliberately to bring Episcopacy in again, as a curb on what he considered the insolence of the ministers, and as a useful instrument of kingcraft.

He proceeded cautiously, and began by putting out a great number of questions, important and unimportant, on ecclesiastical discipline and policy, for the consideration of a General Assembly. This he summoned for February, 1597, at Perth, where the northern ministers could more conveniently gather. It was· more amenable regarding pulpit censures and excommunications than Assemblies dominated by the Edinburgh ministers. Another Assembly was held after three months at Dundee, and James, professing his anxiety to see a minister

settled in every parish, and a stipend assigned to
every minister, procured the appointment of a standing Commission of fourteen prominent ministers.
This Commission possessed considerable powers but
was constantly under the royal influence, and became
the king's stalking-horse. To the commissioners,
and through them, he began to moot the question
of the Church's representation in Parliament. In
another General Assembly, at Dundee in 1598,
he got the principle approved by a majority of
ten. "I wish not," he had said, "to bring in Papistical or Anglican bishops, but only to have the
best and wisest of the ministry appointed by the
General Assembly to have place in Council and
Parliament, to sit upon their own matters and see
them done." But passages from the privately printed
Basilicon Doron, written by King James for his son
Prince Henry, became public, and all James's denials
and explanations could not prevent men from finding
in it a clear determination to uproot Presbyterianism
and to plant Episcopacy in its place.

The General Assembly at Montrose in 1600 was
persuaded to agree that the king should appoint the
Parliamentary Commissioners out of nominees of the
Assembly; and then proceeded to add an enormous
list of *caveats* binding them down to entire sub-
jection to the Assembly. James at last appointed,
at a clerical Convention which he had called, three

bishops to vacant sees of which a fraction of the benefices still existed. Nominal Episcopacy was thus restored; and the Assembly of 1602 resolved that ministers should be appointed to all the bishoprics, and drew up a list of nominees.

When James in 1603 succeeded Queen Elizabeth, and took up his residence in England, not only was his tendency to exalt his prerogative fostered, and his inclination towards Episcopacy strengthened, but his actual power in Scotland was increased. He was beyond the reach of the unflattering tongues of Presbyterian ministers. They could not raise popular feeling against him; nor indeed did the most vehement desire to do so. The whole Scottish nation was proud to see its three hundred years' struggle with England concluded by the accession of a Scottish king to the English crown. The nobles saw fairer fortunes opening before them, and the statesmen a wider sphere of action. The merchants were hoping for an increase in trade. The country was at peace. And it must be said to the credit both of James and of the Church that they had for years wrought harmoniously and successfully in one thing —the allaying of the personal animosities and the family feuds of the Scottish nobles. The Assembly had come to terms with the king; the abuse of free speech in the pulpit and censure in the ecclesiastical courts had been checked; and a spirit of moderation was ruling. Had James been content to carry the Church along with him, he might have gradually established what many have considered an ideal church polity, a Presbyterian Church with a certain amount of superintendence in the hands of ministers specially selected, or an Episcopal Church in which the prelates were regarded as the representatives and executive of the presbyters, the laity also having their place and voice in the Church courts.

But James was false to the profession he had made, and set himself, first, to silence the rigid Presbyterians, then to abolish the General Assembly or reduce it to impotence, and to put its power into the hands of the bishops, who were creatures of the king. Uniformity with the Church of England was his avowed ideal for the Scottish Church; and he lost little time in taking steps to that end. The Church in 1603 was Presbyterian in form and in fact; it rested upon the settlement of 1592. It had agreed to check the violence of individual ministers in personal denunciations, and had moderated its zeal in excommunications. This did not affect its polity. But one concession had been made. Certain ministers had been given votes in Parliament under the name of "bishops," though without jurisdiction over their brethren. James determined to make this the germ of a real Episcopacy in the Church. The next Assembly, 1604, was prorogued to 1605, and then again prorogued indefinitely. Annual Assemblies had been guaranteed by the Act of 1592, and the ministers who had gathered to the Assembly in 1605 and constituted it, adjourned it to meet again, claiming the inherent right of the Assembly to do so. Most of them were summoned before the Council and tried by a packed jury, under one of the laws of 1584, for taking part in an unlawful Convocation; six were banished for life and eight exiled to the extremities of the kingdom and to Ireland. Eight other ministers, including Andrew Melville, were summoned to London to confer with the king, and only allowed to return to Scotland under severe restrictions. Melville could not be intimidated; but he was imprisoned in the Tower and finally allowed to retire to France. His nephew James was compelled to remain in England. The party loyal to Presbyterianism as a polity was now silenced.

Meantime the vacant bishoprics had been filled up, and ten bishops sat in the Parliament of 1606. The Act of annexation of their temporalities was repealed, and their estate was restored to what it had been before 1587; while the mouths of the nobles were stopped by the confirmation of what they had gained under that Act, and seventeen prelacies were erected in their favour into temporal lordships. A Convention was summoned of laymen and ministers nominated by the king, and it agreed that every presbytery should have a "constant moderator," with a pension from the Crown. Year by year royal declarations, "General Assemblies" nominated by the Crown, and Acts of Parliament increased the power and jurisdiction of the bishops, and diminished the authority of the Presbyteries.

But James's bishops were still only Presbyterian ministers elevated to dignity and authority by the civil power; they wanted the genuine Episcopal stamp. Three of them, including Spottiswoode, the primate, were therefore summoned to London in 1610, and consecrated by the bishops of London, Ely, and Bath. Andrewes, Bishop of Ely, at first wished to have them ordained priests, as their ordination had only been by Presbyters. But Bancroft, Archbishop of Canterbury, anti-puritan though he was, would not agree to a principle which would deny lawful ordination in most of the Reformed churches. And Abbot, Bishop of London, quoted cases like that of Ambrose of Milan, in which laymen had been at once consecrated as bishops. The three Scotsmen were therefore consecrated bishops, and on their return to Scotland consecrated the others.

Finally, in 1612 the great Act of 1592 was repealed, and the Church of Scotland was an openly Episcopal Church. Lordly prelates sat in Parliament held their courts of High Commission, presided in their synods, and controlled all important acts of Church order and discipline.

But Presbyterianism was not dead. It survived as a doctrine and an ideal in the minds of many ministers and of many laymen as well. It lived and acted in the Kirk Sessions where ministers and elders jealously controlled the religion and morals of the people.

James had not dared to dissolve the Presbyteries, which continued as before to rule the Church, though under more or less direction from the bishop or his deputy, and no longer constituted in part of laymen. The doctrine, discipline, and worship of the Church remained as before; and so long as these things were untouched the people were little moved by the appointment of bishops, or even by their consecration with all its ecclesiastical implications. The Church of 1612 was not unpopular and might well have become permanent, though it had been set up by acts of tyranny and stretches of the prerogative. Such men as David Lindsay, one of the little band of preachers of 1560 and Bishop of Ross since 1600, who died in extreme old age in 1613, were not likely to be found among the prelates of an oppressive Church.

But James did not know when to stop; and he proceeded, against the advice of his own bishops, to measures which raised popular odium against the

order which he had established.   The Church was
passionately anti-papal; and Protestantism, for the
mass of the people, was bound up with the worship
and usages which for fifty years had represented
Protestantism to them.   The king revisited Scotland
in 1617, and in Holyrood Chapel Royal the Anglican
service was set up, and the bishops, the Council, and
the nobles ordered to take part in it, even to the
length of kneeling at Communion, instead of sitting
at the table.   An Act of Parliament was proposed
which would have abolished General Assemblies, but
the king did not venture to press it, though he
punished some protesting ministers.   He would fain
have pressed certain Anglican usages upon the whole
Church, and the bishops reluctantly undertook to
have them brought before and put through a General
Assembly.   A carefully packed Assembly was called at
Perth in 1618, an absurd, insolent, and tyrannical letter
from the king was read, and James's "Five Articles"
were forced through, largely by the votes of the laity
who had been summoned.   But even in a gathering
which had the merest pretence to represent the
Church, such opposition had been offered to the
royal will that James determined to have done with
Assemblies.   No other met until 1638, and then it
met not to please but to defy a king.

The Five Articles of Perth seem to many modern
Presbyterians not very offensive and partly laudable

in matter. They enjoined (1) Kneeling at Communion; (2) Private Communion for the sick; (3) Private Baptism where public was inconvenient; (4) Confirmation by the bishop of children at the age of eight; (5) Observance of the five chief holy days. But they seemed to many in 1618 the beginning of a return to Rome, and they were known by all to be an attempt to assimilate the Church of Scotland to that of England at the will of the monarch. Protestant feeling, patriotic resentment, and the spirit of free men united to spurn what reason and toleration might in time have made, in part, acceptable. The Five Articles were never acted upon throughout the Church. Even the bishops as a body were not hearty about them. But they were the law, for they were ratified by Parliament in 1621. Their enforcement became the cause of strife and persecution in many a Presbytery. The Church became confused in its worship. As Knox had foreseen, liberty and order were bound up with free Assemblies. Moreover, the mass of the laity were now concerned about the change in usages which were for them an integral part of their religion, and a spirit of discontent began to pervade the land.

James VI died in 1625, and was succeeded by Charles, a prince with an equally high idea of his prerogative and with an equal zeal and more real veneration for the Church in its Anglican form.

Scottish ministers in vain petitioned him for relief from the Perth Articles; Charles regarded these as only a first step in the Anglicizing of the Scottish Church. The bishops he appointed were, many of them, Scots in English orders, and their spirit was the spirit of Laud, comparatively liberal in doctrine, addicted to ritual, intolerant of opposition, and unsympathetic with the characteristics of the Reformation Church in Scotland.

Charles had a regard for the decent maintenance of the clergy, as indeed his father also had in an intermittent fashion; and one of his first acts—a revocation of all Crown grants made during the two preceding reigns, including all Church lands—was meant to provide for the ministry, as well as to produce revenue for the Crown. This sweeping measure was so modified by later concessions and compositions that it ended in giving each minister something like a living wage out of the teinds of his own parish. It put the teinds back in the hands of the actual landowners in the parish, instead of in those of some great lord who had held them with the benefice to which they had been annexed and which he was still permitted to hold of the king. The lords really lost little but the power of annoying the clergy and the lairds. But they had been threatened; and this one excellent Act of Charles's reign was not counted to him for righteousness in the minds of the Scottish nobility.

In 1633 Charles came to be crowned in Edinburgh, Laud, Bishop of London, accompanying him. An elaborate service after the Anglican fashion was held in the Chapel Royal, and the coronation service itself was managed, though, of course, not conducted, by Laud. To the great irritation of the citizens the English service was used in St Giles's Church itself. The royal prerogative in ecclesiastical matters was strengthened by Act of Parliament, not without protest by ministers and laymen, and the arrangements as to Church lands and teinds were confirmed by law. Having erected Edinburgh into a bishopric and endowed it, Charles returned to England, leaving behind him a considerable ferment of dissatisfaction with his policy, and a growing grudge against the bishops as instruments of the king's absolutism. This feeling was aggravated when in 1635 Archbishop Spottiswoode was made lord chancellor in succession to a layman. Undeterred, nevertheless, by the evident uneasiness and indisposition of his Scottish subjects to submit to innovations, Charles in 1636 issued a Book of "Canons and Constitutions" for the Church of Scotland, in which, without warrant ecclesiastical or parliamentary, and by his own royal will, he transformed the rites and government of the Church, and even touched the civil law. The country was seething with resentment. Finally, in May, 1637, appeared a Book of Common Prayer, made compulsory by an Act of Privy Council.

The patience of the Scottish people was exhausted. At the mere word of the king, every Scotsman was to have his worship altered. Knox's Liturgy was to be displaced by Laud's, and the minister's freedom of "conceived" prayer, which was permitted by the former and widely used, was to be exchanged for bondage to a form of words dictated by Anglicans, and more "popish" than the Anglican Liturgy itself. Other innovations had touched the laity but occasionally; this interfered with their "use and wont" and upset their weekly worship, wantonly, illegally, and offensively. And, moreover, was it not, men asked, simply the beginning of the restoration of popery?

On Sunday, the 23rd of July, 1637, in St Giles's Church, the chief dignitaries of the realm being present, the Dean of Edinburgh began to read the new book, and in a moment the Church was in an uproar. Edinburgh would have none of Laud's Liturgy. Nor would Scotland generally. In vain were demonstrations against the bishops and the Service-Book prohibited on pain of death by the Privy Council. Its use had to be suspended. Petitions against the Service-Book came pouring in. But Charles did not grasp the gravity of the situation, and avowed himself as the person responsible for the Liturgy. Nobles, lairds, burgesses, and ministers gathered together in Edinburgh; and tables, or committees, each representing one of these classes, were appointed to manage the agitation. Its scope widened with Charles's delays. The Episcopate, and all recent innovations, now became objects of attack. The enthusiasm grew, and at last a National Covenant was drawn up—the King's Confession of 1581, a recital of the Acts of Parliament confirming it, a statement of recent changes as violating it, and an oath of mutual support in defence of the Crown and of true religion. Beginning in Greyfriars Church, Edinburgh, on the 28th of February, 1638, the signing of the Covenant went on over all Scotland. The great majority of all classes who could sign at all concurred in it, though certain districts in the north were backward. The will of the people was unmistakeable. "Now," said Archbishop Spottiswoode, "all that we have been doing these thirty years past is thrown down at once." With most of his colleagues, he took refuge in England. Episcopacy was overthrown; and all that remained to be done was to put a legal seal to an accomplished fact.

CHAPTER V

CHARLES was at last compelled to recognize that he had to deal with a national revolt, not against the king, indeed, but against the ecclesiastical system which he and his father had set up and the absolutism which had established it. The Covenanters called for a free Assembly and a meeting of the Estates; and the use they intended to make of them was no secret. After protracted negotiations through the Marquis of Hamilton and others—the Covenanters' demands rising higher every month—the king agreed, under conditions, that a General Assembly should be held on the 21st of November, 1638.

The election of members was, in most cases, made in accordance with the instructions of the Tables. Against the wish even of many Covenanting ministers, but by a revival of the old practice and law of the

Church, an elder from each Kirk Session took his seat in the Presbytery of the bounds, and voted for the representatives, clerical as well as lay, whom the Presbytery were entitled to send to the Assembly. At this stage, the laity were more thorough-going than the clergy ; and the result was an Assembly whose members were mostly pledged beforehand to extreme measures. It met at Glasgow on the appointed date. Of the 240 members, 98 were elders, of whom 17 were noblemen. Alexander Henderson, minister of Leuchars, was appointed Moderator. Hamilton, the King's Commissioner, pronounced the Assembly dissolved when it insisted on considering the question of Episcopacy, and withdrew. Undeterred by this, the Assembly abjured Episcopacy and all the innovations connected with it, declared all pretended Assemblies since 1605 null and void, tried all the bishops for violating the *caveats* upon which they had been appointed and many of them for crimes of which the slenderest evidence was offered, deposed all the fourteen from the ministry and excommunicated eight. (Three of them ultimately took the Covenant and became parish ministers, after being restored.) The Assembly then restored Presbyterian government,·and fortified it by various Acts. After a month's labour, it was closed.

Then the country prepared for war. The Assembly had acted "treasonably" in acting at all after

Hamilton's withdrawal, and was ready to take the consequences. Charles was known to have been preparing long before. The succeeding events belong to civil history and can have but the briefest notice here. Finding the forces which he was able to gather unfit to face the Covenanting army in battle, Charles again consented to allow a free General Assembly and a meeting of the Estates. The Edinburgh Assembly of 1639 confirmed the Acts of the Glasgow Assembly, and the Estates would have ratified them, but were delayed by the king's procrastination and finally by being prorogued till 1640. In June 1640 the Estates met, refused, on a technical plea, to recognize a further prorogation, and confirmed what had been done by the preceding Assembly. Again the country prepared for war, and the army marched into England, not however in any hostile way. For now England was also stirring. That country had its grievances against the king, and was demanding redress with irresistible voice. The Short Parliament of 1640 had been dissolved without voting Charles money for the war; the Parliament, later to be called the Long Parliament, met in November; and soon Charles had two angry kingdoms upon his hands. But if Scotland were appeased, it might aid him to overawe his restive subjects in England. He therefore accepted the situation so far as Scotland was concerned, came to Edinburgh, and gave full

Royal and Parliamentary sanction to all the measures
which had made Scotland again a Presbyterian
country. In November, 1641, Charles returned south,
"a contented king from a contented country." The
ecclesiastical revolution had ended in a complete and
lawful settlement.

But it came too late for the peace of Scotland.
The Civil War in England broke out in the following
year, and Scotland was inevitably involved. Since
Knox's days there had been much sympathy in the
Church of Scotland with Englishmen who desired relief
from many of the ceremonies of the English Church ;
and in recent years the sufferers under Anglican
Episcopacy were naturally the friends of Scottish
Presbyterianism. And the three years, from 1638
to 1641, had wrought a change, in some respects for
the worse, in Scottish feeling. A country threatened
with the loss of its liberties and ideals and determined to maintain them is apt to grow intolerant
of dissidents in its midst, suspicious of neutrals,
narrow in its views, and fanatical in its devotion to
the symbols of its unity and freedom. The Covenant
had become almost a fetish and often an instrument
of oppression. Scores of non-covenanting ministers
had been deposed and expelled from their charges ;
zealots of a rigid, bitter and enthusiastic type were
changing the temper of the Church, and the Church
was now almost omnipotent. Yet loyalty to the

king and an unwillingness to enter on a fratricidal
strife kept Scotland neutral for a time, even after
the outbreak of the Civil War. But ecclesiastical
ambition for the assertion of the *jus divinum* of
Presbytery, and perhaps fear of the untrusted king,
who seemed for a time to be gaining the upper hand,
at last determined Scotland to accept the overtures
of the English Parliament. The General Assembly
and the Convention of Estates in Scotland, the
Houses of Parliament and the Westminster Assembly
of Divines in England, entered into a Solemn League
and Covenant for the reformation of religion in
England and Ireland and its preservation in Scotland,
and for the defence of the privileges of Parliament
and the person and authority of the king. Scotland
confidently looked for the extension of Presbytery to
both the neighbouring kingdoms. A Scottish army
again crossed the Tweed. The Parliamentary cause,
strengthened by this alliance, gradually became vic-
torious, and in May, 1646, Charles rode into the
quarters of the Scottish army a beaten king.

Presbyterianism seemed to be on the point of
triumph ; the work of the Solemn League and
Covenant seemed near completion. The Westminster
Assembly of Divines, aided by Scots Commissioners,
had drawn up a Form of Church Government and
a Directory for Public Worship, which had been
received and approved by the General Assembly ;

and now it pressed on with the completion of its
Confession of Faith, which, with its Longer and
Shorter Catechisms, was also received by the Scottish
Church. The Form of Church Government was
practically an acceptance of Presbyterianism in its
Scottish form. But the Directory repudiated fixed
liturgical forms, and its acceptance hastened the dis-
appearance of the old Scottish Book of Common
Order. This Liturgy, indeed, was already being set
aside by the more enthusiastic ministers, who would
not pray but as they were "moved by the Spirit."
The movement against the rigid Laudian form thus
carried away with it the ancient monument of Reformation devotion. The ancient Confession, without
being repudiated or treated disrespectfully, also sank
into disuse before the longer, more logical, more
definite, but narrower and more purely intellectual
Confession of Westminster. Scotland subordinated
her historical testimony, and suffered alteration in
her national worship, for the sake of uniformity ; she
even adopted a new metrical version of the psalms ;
with the singular result that in the end the Westminster documents, which were in the main the work
of English Puritans, have become the peculiar possession of the Church of Scotland and her daughter
churches. Her loss, as against her gain, who can
compute ? Yet who that reckons the loss as greater
will deny the partial compensation in intellectual and
religious training furnished to so many generations

of Scottish youth by the best known of the Westminster formularies, the Shorter Catechism?

A sad disillusionment awaited the Church. The
English army, full of enthusiastic sectaries, would not
follow the lead of the Parliament, still predominantly
Presbyterian. It pressed for greater toleration, and
also for its arrears of pay. Charles saw, or thought
he saw, his opportunity, and intrigued with all the
parties, while faithful to none. At last he entered
into an "Engagement" with Scottish Commissioners,
making many concessions to Presbyterianism and
the promise of a free Parliament. A Scottish army
entered England under the Marquis of Hamilton, but
it met with utter rout at the hands of Cromwell at
Preston, in 1648. The "Engagers," moreover, had
not been sufficiently zealous for the Covenant; and
the army had marched at the order of the Estates
but under the ban of the Church. Hamilton's
defeat now gave the Church or Covenanting party
the upper hand. By virtue of the character of
their intense personal religion and of their common hostility to Charles's "malignancy," Cromwell
and the more severe Covenanters for the moment
were at one. But with the execution of Charles
in January, 1649, they fell apart. Scotland was
loyal to her ancient line of kings, and Charles II
was at once proclaimed in Edinburgh. Gathering an
army again, but purging it of all but Covenanters of
the strictest sort, Scotland stood for the Covenants

and Charles II, till Cromwell routed her forces at
Dunbar in 1650. The national disaster and humilia-
tion brought an accession of reasonableness, and with
the goodwill of the Church, another army, more
liberally recruited, marched south in 1651 to try to
raise England for king and freedom. But England
had had enough and would not rise ; and at Worcester
Cromwell finally pulverized the fighting power of the
Scots. From 1651 to 1660 Cromwell and his successors ruled Scotland, justly and not too harshly,
yet practically as a province of England, and that an
"Independent" England, with no love for Presbytery
any more than for Episcopacy. The General Assembly
of 1653 was dispersed, and no other was suffered to
meet. The hopes of 1643 were dismally falsified ; the
Solemn League and Covenant had failed.

Yet Presbyterianism lived on. The inferior
courts continued to meet, worship to be conducted,
and discipline to be administered. Occasional rude-
ness and interruption on the part of Cromwell's
soldiers was a comparatively small thing. More
serious by far was the schism which now manifested
itself publicly in the Church. The greater part of
the clergy were "Resolutioners," having concurred in
the resolutions which had received into the army in
the final struggle for "life, religion, king and freedom" former "malignants," who had once fought
for the king against the Estates and the Church and

the Covenant. The minority were "Protesters," who protested against the smallest defection from absolute loyalty to the Covenants and unswerving severity to all its enemies and gainsayers. They declined to sit in the same courts with the Resolutioners, separated themselves and set up opposition courts, and struck at a fundamental principle of Presbyterianism by ignoring the vote of a majority whenever it chanced to be against what the "godly" preferred. This spirit, tending to individualism, if not to utter anarchy, was more akin to that of Cromwell's soldiers than the spirit of the Resolutioners ; and so was the Protesters' vehement outcry against the sins of the royal family. Naturally, therefore, the Protesting clergy were more favoured by the English rulers than were the Resolutioners ; and the Scots laymen associated with the English in the government of the country were of the same stamp.

Without the unifying and controlling influence of a General Assembly strange developments of religion took place, more especially where the Protesters were strong. Fasts before the Sacrament of the Lord's Supper were instituted, great gatherings of preachers and people took place, and the sacramental season, covering the greater part of a week, was mainly occupied by an almost unintermittent series of sermons. Sermons and prayers became portentously long. Preachers assumed a rhapsodical, exalted, and un-

natural manner of speech ; and religious excitement
was allowed to run uncontrolled. Of the fervent
piety and rigid morality of most of the extremists
there can be no reasonable doubt ; of their bigotry
and unreasonableness there can be as little. The
Covenants usurped the place of the Gospel as the
guide at least of their civil life ; and in their devotions they had cast aside the order which three
generations of Scottish Protestants had observed.
English Puritanism as well as English Episcopacy has
deeply affected, and not entirely for good, the course
of Scottish Church history, in respect that the influence of each has, in its own way, tended to obscure
the genius of the national type.

In 1660 came the triumphant return of Charles II
to England. Scotland's miserable condition had been
the result of its determination to be loyal both to
the king and to the Covenants. Its king was now
restored ; what of its Covenant and its Church ? The
renewal of the Covenant was forbidden ; Argyll and
Guthrie, lay and clerical leaders of the extremists,
were seized, tried for treason, condemned and
executed. But Charles had promised to preserve
the government of the Church as settled by law,
and the mass of people in Scotland, taught wisdom
by their misfortunes, would have welcomed a return
to an uncovenanted Presbyterianism, even though
a strong regal prerogative should bridle its excesses.

But restrained by no scruple and misled by bad
advice, Charles proceeded to restore Episcopacy.
The "Drunken Parliament" of 1661 passed an Act
Rescissory, destroying the whole legislation since 1633,
thus taking away the legal standing of Presbyterianism
and providing Charles with the pretext that Episcopacy was now the form of government of the Church
recognized by law. Once more were Anglican
bishops called upon to consecrate Scottish ministers
to the Episcopate. Two of them—James Sharp and
Robert Leighton—had been ordained since 1638, and
were therefore in Presbyterian orders. The Anglicans
had grown narrower since 1610, and insisted that
these Presbyterian ministers should first be ordained
deacons and priests before being raised to Episcopal
rank. Leighton did not demur, but it was a bitter
pill for Sharp to swallow. He had, however, to
swallow it; and that after a remonstrance which only
served to show his character in its true light; the
Archbishopric of St Andrews, which gilded the pill,
was too great a bribe for the man who had been sent
to Charles as the spokesman for the Presbyterianism
of Scotland and had betrayed his trust. The consecrated four returned to Scotland; the remaining
Episcopal sees were filled and their occupants consecrated. The Parliament of 1662 put the whole Church
government into their hands and rescinded all laws
in favour of Presbyterianism, especially the Act of

1592. It brought them back to Parliament as the Spiritual Estate, and gave them the rights and privileges enjoyed before 1638. It made the Covenants treasonable, and exacted from public officers a declaration abjuring them.

A royal proclamation had already forbidden Synods, Presbyteries, and even Kirk Sessions to meet until authorized by the bishops; so that when they did meet, it was as Episcopal courts. But their practical working remained as before, though the chairmanship and control of business remained with the prelates, who also took the place of the General Assembly as the authorized exponents of the Church's mind. A book of Canons was spoken of, but the project came to nothing. No attempt was made to reintroduce either Laud's or Knox's liturgy. Some of the bishops endeavoured to restore a more fixed and orderly form to public worship; but generally without effect. Psalm singing, extempore prayers, reading of scripture with exposition, and sermons formed henceforth the service of the Church of Scotland, though Episcopalians usually forbore exposition, and used the Doxology and the Lord's Prayer. Nor was any attempt made at this time to frame a new Confession of Faith. Knox's Confession held, as it had done since 1560, parliamentary authority; and the Westminster Confession had the adhesion of most of the clergy. In fact Charles and his advisers were not aiming at ecclesiastical improvements, but at establishing the royal supremacy.

Scotland was weary of strife; many even of the Protesters had given over protesting; the clergy were anxious for the unity and efficiency of the Church; the nobility had long ago wearied of the Covenant which had brought them to the brink of ruin; secure now in their possessions, they were well content to see the power of the ministers curbed by the bishops. In spite of the shameful manner of its re-planting in Scotland, Episcopacy would probably have taken root again, had the ground been gradually and carefully occupied. But harsh and violent measures were at once taken to uproot the Covenanting interest. And it was the persecutions which culminated in the "killing time" that finally discredited Episcopacy in the minds of the people of Scotland, and established Presbytery in their hearts as well as in the constitution of the country.

In 1649, at the height of their power, the Church and Parliament had abolished the ancient right of patrons to present to livings, and had placed it in the hands of the Kirk Sessions with the approval of the people. Parliament now ordered all ministers so settled to receive presentation from the patrons, and institution from the bishops. Overwhelmed by the calamities and confusions of the last ten years, and deprived of the means of collective action through a

General Assembly, the ministers had hitherto accepted the new situation without open resistance. But now they were called to own the unlawfulness of their ministry; the sticking-point was reached; and nearly 300 ministers, being the majority of those ordained or translated since 1649 and one-third of the entire ministry of the Church, refused compliance and had to give up their livings in November 1662. Many regions in the south and west were left spiritually desolate. A swarm of ignorant and despicable youths, chiefly from the north, took their places; but the hearts of the people were with their old pastors, and while the parish churches were empty, the open-air preachings of the "outed" ministers were attended by crowds. Parliament then set ruinously heavy fines upon non-attendance at the parish churches; the new "curates" became informers and dragoons the enforcers of the new law.

The violence of the dragoons at last led to a local rising; the armed peasants of the south and west marched towards Edinburgh, but were beaten and dispersed at Rullion Green, among the Pentland Hills; and thirty or forty were executed (1665). The hand of the persecutor was laid upon the "conventicles" and those who attended them more heavily than ever, until the consequences began to trouble even the hardened members of the Privy Council. At last, in 1669, an Indulgence was granted by royal

favour to the ejected ministers, and they were permitted to be appointed to vacant parishes, under
certain conditions. Some forty accepted the conditions, but the remainder condemned their action as
a sinful compliance and a desertion of the Covenant ;
while the bishops, on the other hand, condemned the
Indulgence as both foolish and Erastian. Their answer
came in an Assertory Act which made all matters of
Church government depend entirely upon the will of
the king, a most astounding piece of legislation to
the mind of anyone who does not believe that the
Church is merely a piece of State machinery and the
king the sole fabricant of the mechanism.

Leighton, now Archbishop of Glasgow, a man
whose name should be mentioned with great respect,
attempted to bring the Presbyterians to an accommodation with Episcopacy. But neither were they willing
to give up their Presbyterianism, nor had they reason
to believe that the scheme would be permitted to
become permanent. The gradual encroachments of
Episcopacy and absolutism in the reigns of James VI
and Charles I could not be forgotten. Distrusted by
his Presbyterian opponents and wounded in the house
of his friends by the jealousy as well as the violence
of the bishops, Leighton at last resigned his charge,
and went to end his days in England.

To the end of the reign of Charles II the same
policy was pursued. There was ever-increasing

severity against the stricter Covenanters who refused
to conform and who frequented field-meetings, and
occasional offers of indulgence to Presbyterian ministers who would minister peaceably, and under severe
conditions, in the parish churches. The majority of
the "outed" ministers who survived were at last
preaching under some such recognition. Against the
absolutely non-conforming penal laws of a monstrous
character were passed. To preach and finally even
to attend a conventicle was made punishable by death
(though this offence without further aggravation
was not actually so treated). Husbands were made
responsible for their wives, and landlords for their
tenants; and enormous fines were levied on such as
were unable or unwilling to prevent their respective
charges from attending an occasional field-preaching.
In 1678 ten thousand armed men, of whom 6,000
were rude Highlanders, were quartered for months
in Ayrshire and Clydesdale to enforce this law, and
returned laden with the spoil of the countryside.
Torture was used in the examination of prisoners
before the Privy Council; and means of inflicting it,
hitherto unknown to Scotland, were introduced to
bend the rigid Covenanters to the king's will.

Oppression drove men mad; and some of them
were men who sincerely believed in the Old Testament way of dealing with the tyrants over the people
of God. Archbishop Sharp was murdered in 1679.

Almost simultaneously a blaze sprang up in the west country. An armed conventicle successfully repulsed three troops of horse at Drumclog; and the victors gathered the likeminded into an army to fight for the Covenant. It was beaten at Bothwell Bridge; and the fate of the prisoners was cruel.

Still a few field preachers remained, and an indomitable though scattered band of followers, for thousands of men were actually outlawed for their covenanting practices. These Society-men, or Cameronians (so-called from one of their last leaders, Richard Cameron, who was killed in a skirmish in 1680) spurned all concessions which their weaker brethren made in the way of compliance with the Government. They disowned the apostate king, waged war upon him and his officers, and finally excommunicated him. Yet even among themselves there were those who condemned this last extremity.

Charles died in 1685, and James VII, an acknowledged Roman Catholic, came to the throne. The "killing-time" was at its height. Not defiant Covenanters only, but any who sheltered them, sympathized with them, or refused to abjure their tenets or take humiliating oaths, were victims of relentless persecution. Yet still another Indulgence was offered. James's first step to the restoration of Romanism was the suspension of the penal laws against Roman Catholics and their worship; and what was granted to Papists could not be denied to Presbyterians, unless of the most violent kind. Legal toleration for his co-religionists James could not obtain ; the servile Estates and the crown-made bishops of Scotland were as rankly anti-Romanist as the Cameronians. But he used the royal dispensing power to the utmost, and many non-conforming ministers now preached openly in meeting-houses, only the Cameronians refusing to have anything to do with a Papist king's indulgence. Renwick, their principal preacher, was seized in February 1688 and hanged. But before the end of the year James himself was a fugitive. William of Orange had landed in England to deliver both kingdoms from religious and civil despotism, exercised in the interest of the hated and dreaded Roman Catholicism. His arrival brought instant relief to the persecuted Presbyterians of Scotland. But for a time Episcopacy and Presbytery hung balanced in the scales, until their long strife was brought to a decisive conclusion by the Revolution Settlement.

CHAPTER VI

THE REVOLUTION SETTLEMENT AND THE UNION:
1689—1707

WILLIAM OF ORANGE was himself a member of a Presbyterian Church. His principal adviser in Scottish matters was William Carstares, a Presbyterian minister, who had suffered imprisonment and torture for his political and religious principles, and had found a refuge in Holland. Holland was full of Scottish refugees, enemies of James's despotism civil and religious, and Presbyterians to a man. William therefore landed in England with a predisposition in favour of re-establishing Presbyterianism in Scotland and a preconception of its wide popularity in that country. His Declaration, however, while outspoken on the point of preserving the Protestant religion, and of vindicating the laws and liberties of the country, was cautiously silent as to Presbyterianism. In London William came into touch with many

Scottish nobles and the spokesmen of the bishops, and found that Episcopacy had a strong following among the classes who had political importance. His position in England, moreover, derived its strength from the alienation of the Church of England from the Romanist James ; and William was naturally anxious to retain the support of that Church. The maintenance of Episcopacy in Scotland would undoubtedly conciliate even strong Anglicans, and had the Scottish episcopate given him the same encouragement as the English, he might have given it his support. But the bishops gave him to understand that they were not prepared to consent to his being made king in the place of James. William therefore left the whole matter to be settled by Scotland for herself.

Scotland had done with James. And since the bishops would not give him up many of their lay supporters gave them up. The Scottish Convention of Estates, elected, so far as the representatives of the shires and the burghs were concerned, on an unusually wide and free basis, declared (April 1689) that James had forfeited the crown, and they passed a claim of Right stating the grievances of the country, and declaring William and Mary King and Queen. In this document the declaration was made "That Prelacy and the superiority of any office in the Church above Presbyters is, and hath been, a great and unsupportable grievance and trouble to this nation, and contrary to the inclination of the generality of the people, ever since the Reformation (they having reformed from Popery by Presbyters) and therefore ought to be abolished." On that basis the crown of Scotland was received by William and Mary. The Scottish bishops had embraced the principles of the Stewart kings, and now they were cast off with the Stewarts as an incubus on the nation. Prelacy was legally abolished in the ensuing Parliament of 1689; the bishops ceased to sit in Parliament or to control the Church courts, which now met with their Moderators chosen in the old Presbyterian fashion. But the General Assembly, in abeyance since 1653—the common dread of Cromwell and the Stewarts—could not immediately be restored. A Presbyterian General Assembly can hardly be evoked from a meeting of Episcopal clergy, who hold strong Episcopalian views. And such was the case with most of the clergy in 1689, who were in this respect unlike their predecessors in 1638. A change in the *personnel* was necessary.

Such a change had in part been made already. On the news of William's landing reaching Scotland, the Cameronians and their sympathizers in the south-west had "rabbled the curates," i.e. ejected the Episcopal ministers who had been the agents or informers of the Government in its repressive measures, and whom the lapse of 28 years had not taught how to gain the affection or respect of the people. Further, the Convention of 1689 had enjoined public prayers to be made for the new king and queen instead of for James, and the Privy Council had deprived more than 180 ministers for disobedience. But still more had to be done.

The Parliament of 1690 grasped the nettle firmly. It passed one Act abolishing the Supremacy Act of 1669, another restoring the Presbyterian ministers who had been expelled since 1661, and another ratifying the Westminster Confession of Faith as the doctrine of the Church of Scotland, restoring Presbyterian Church government on the basis of the Act of 1592, empowering the restored ministers and the ministers and elders whom they should associate with themselves to govern and purge the church, and declaring vacant the parishes from which the Episcopal ministers had been either "rabbled" or legally expelled.

Sixty-one venerable ministers remained of the hundreds who had been expelled under Charles II. In putting the whole ecclesiastical power in their hands, the State had, in the fullest way, made the *amende honorable* for its former action, and had invested them with a great responsibility and trust. On the whole, they used it moderately. With some other old ministers, Presbyterian in sympathy, some young men recently ordained, and a number of elders, they formed a General Assembly 180 strong. The three surviving Cameronian ministers were received into the Church, though a band of lay irreconcilables refused to own a non-covenanting settlement; attempts to resuscitate the controversies of the old days of the covenanting supremacy were decisively put down; useful legislation for the religious work of the Church was passed; and two commissions were appointed to purge the Church, north and south, including the Universities.

A degree of harshness characterized the proceedings of the commissions; and William became uneasy. He would fain have seen such Episcopalian ministers retained as would conform to the new order in Church and State. But the next Assembly, in 1692, was unwilling to admit to the courts of the Church men who, they feared, would use their position to subvert the system with which they promised concurrence. William's Commissioner dissolved it with words of strong censure and without summoning another Assembly. But the Moderator, before closing it with prayer, named a day on which the next Assembly would meet. A collision between Church and State was again imminent, between the asserted prerogative by the King as head of the State to summon or leave unsummoned the General Assembly of the National Church, and the freedom claimed by the

Church to hold General Assemblies when it pleased Before the day named by the Moderator had come, the King had seen fit, at the request of Parliament, to summon an Assembly, for a later day indeed, but still in substantial accord with the Church's claim. Since then there has been an uninterrupted series of annual Assemblies. The recognition of a common interest and mutual obligation and the dictates of prudence and common-sense thus closed one phase of a century's friction, with occasional conflict, between Church and State.

The Parliament of 1693, whose intervention prevented a collision between William and the Church, passed an important "Act for settling the Quiet and Peace of the Church." It was intended to facilitate the admission of Episcopal ministers who should take the oaths of allegiance and assurance, subscribe the Westminster Confession of Faith, owning it as the confession of their faith, accept and loyally maintain the Presbyterian government, and observe uniformity of worship as at present in use. Indeed, it was for the orderly admission of such that the Assembly had to be called. But, incidentally, this Act settled for the Church up to the present time part, at least, of the promises which every candidate for the ministry must take before receiving ordination.

After preliminary negotiations of a delicate and critical character, the Assembly of 1694 accordingly met and agreed to receive Episcopal ministers who fully conformed, and who acknowledged William as king *de jure* as well as *de facto*. Finally, an Act of Parliament in 1695 protected in their livings, though without a place in the Church judicatories, all the Episcopal ministers who took the requisite declaration and oath of allegiance. Thus the Church absorbed all who were fit and willing to enter her full ministry as loyal to her faith and polity, and the State protected all the others who were loyal to the State. Some contrived to remain in possession without conforming to either. At the Union of the crowns in 1707, Episcopal ministers were still serving in 165 out of the 900 parishes of the Church, the survivors of probably double that number who held out against conformity with Presbyterianism in 1690, and yet did not forfeit their livings or their functions.

In spite of " rabblings " of unpopular ministers, of legal ejectments of men who refused to acknowledge the new monarchs, of occasional narrow-minded " purging " of men whose only fault was attachment to Episcopacy, the Revolution Settlement was, on the whole, a tolerant settlement. This may be attributed in part to the general feeling of Scotsmen that while Episcopacy must be done away with as unpopular in itself and a tool in the hands of a tyrannical and persecuting government, it would be absurd and iniquitous to permit extremists for the Covenants to retaliate in kind. Something also must be attributed to the sixty-one old ministers, exiled, or silenced, or indulged, who when restored and clothed with such extended powers, showed that suffering had taught them reasonableness and a measure of charity. Nor must the labours of Leighton and his school be forgotten ; the Church of Scotland at last reaped what they had sown. But, above all, justice must be done to William of Orange. When the crown of Scotland was offered to him, with uplifted hands he repeated the words of the Coronation oath, until that clause was read which bound him to "root out heretics and enemies of the true worship of God." Then William paused and said, "I will not lay myself under any obligation to be a persecutor." And only when his protest was accepted would he proceed. Many as were the just grievances which his administration of Scottish affairs created, Scotland owes much to the monarch who re-established Presbyterianism and more to him in respect that he tempered it with toleration.

As the Act of 1690, and the proceedings centring round it, made a final settlement of most of the controversies which had agitated the Church since the Reformation, and as subsequent history has produced little alteration on the relations of Church and State or on the constitution of the Church thereby established, it may be well to note here, in a summary way, the salient points of the situation now attained.

1.   Presbyterian government by Kirk Sessions, Presbyteries, Provincial Synods, and General Assemblies was fully restored.   These courts again became the ecclesiastical courts of the country, with the right to call in the aid of the civil power to make their jurisdiction effective.

2.   The Church was left free and autonomous within its own freely-chosen constitution, the crown having no power of interference in any of its actions (unless, of course, any of its courts transgressed beyond the ecclesiastical province), and having no power of appointment of any of its ministers or officials.   On the other hand, churchmen ceased to sit in parliament or to hold civil offices.   Thus Church and State had their jurisdictions delimited and their provinces separated.

3.   The link between the State and the Church continued to be the King, as represented by his Lord High Commissioner.   The procedure fixed shortly after the Revolution continues to this day.   The Lord High Commissioner attends the General Assembly and sits on a throne ; but the Moderator chosen by the Assembly is the Chairman.   At the last sitting the Assembly fixes the time and place for the meeting of the next Assembly, and the Moderator having intimated this, thereafter dissolves the Assembly in the

name of the Lord Jesus Christ, the Head of the
Church. The Commissioner also, in the King's name,
intimates the next and dissolves the sitting Assembly.
This working compromise, or rather agreement, by
which both summon a General Assembly for the same
time and place, closed the long-standing controversy
regarding freedom of Assemblies and the power of
the Christian prince.

4. The Westminster Confession of Faith, read
at full length to a weary Parliament, became the
doctrine of the Church as recognized by the State.
The older Scots Confession sank out of sight. The
other Westminster documents were not read in
Parliament and did not become part of the constitution of the Church recognized and guaranteed by the
State.

5. The Covenants were not recognized by the
State. They were not even renewed by the Church.
The Solemn League and Covenant was manifestly
incompatible with the Revolution Settlement in
England. Even the National Covenant could fall
into desuetude now that the essentials of the Church's
claims were embodied in an Act of Parliament.
Nevertheless, ecclesiastical constitutional purists
continued then and long after to maintain that the
Covenants were binding on the Church, if not on the
State also, as the Cameronians held.

6. The *jus divinum* of Presbytery was not recog-

nized by the State. The Act of 1690 was intended to settle "the government of Christ's Church within the nation, agreeable to the word of God and most conducive to the advancement of true piety and godliness and the establishing of peace and tranquillity within this realm," and it therefore ratified the establishment of Presbyterian Church government, as settled by the Act of 1592 "and thereafter received by the general consent of this nation, to be the only government of Christ's Church within this Kingdom." The Commission of Assembly of 1698, for the satisfaction of uneasy members of the Church, published a mild "Seasonable Admonition" in which Presbyterian Church government was declared to be that instituted by Christ; and then the matter was allowed to slumber.

7. In one respect the legislation of 1690 set aside and went beyond the Act of 1592. That Act had recognized the rights of patrons to present ministers to presbyteries for induction to parishes ; now it was provided that the heritors (i.e. landowners who paid teinds in the parish) and elders should present a person for the approval of the congregation, and that if the congregation objected, the matter should be decided by the presbytery. This was not merely a concession to high presbyterian principles, but a safeguard against the presentation of Episcopal ministers by like-minded patrons, for many of the nobility of Scotland in 1690 were still Episcopal in

sympathy.   As will be seen, this part of the Revolution Settlement was ere long unsettled again, with dire results.

8.   A fertile source of troubles was destroyed by an Act of the Parliament of 1712 which forbade any civil penalty to follow excommunication.   While this Act undoubtedly withdrew a kind of aid which Knox and Melville, as well as their opponents, expected the State to render to the Church, it strengthened immensely their cardinal principle of the independent jurisdictions of the civil and ecclesiastical courts, and purified the discipline of the latter by making it rest simply upon spiritual, or at least ecclesiastical sanctions.

The years succeeding the Revolution Settlement were spent mainly in putting presbyterial machinery into full working order, and in providing for ordinances in neglected and vacant places, particularly in the regions left desolate by a widespread deprivation of Episcopal ministers.   1696 saw a melancholy episode—the execution of an unhappy young student under an Act of Charles II, for blasphemy ; but it was the last of its kind.

In 1697 the General Assembly passed the Act which is known as the " Barrier Act," in regard to which it is worth while to give a short explanation. The General Assembly is supreme over the legislation of the Church.   All proposals for new legislation

8—2

have to be initiated by "overture" either from individuals or from one of the subordinate courts of the Church. The General Assembly of 1639 had ordained that no innovation calculated to disturb the peace of the Church should be "suddenly proposed and enacted." The General Assembly of 1697 " considering the frequent practice of former Assemblies of this Church, and that it will mightily conduce to the exact obedience of the Acts of Assemblies that General Assemblies be very deliberate in making of the same, and that the whole Church have previous knowledge thereof, and for preventing any sudden alteration or innovation or other prejudice of the Church in either doctrine, worship, discipline or government thereof, now happily established; do therefore appoint, enact and declare that before any General Assembly of this Church shall pass any Acts which are to be binding Rules and Constitutions to the Church, the same Acts be first proposed as overtures to the Assembly, and being by them passed as such be remitted to the consideration of the several Presbyteries of this Church," and concludes by providing that unless the majority of the Presbyteries consent, and the next Assembly following agrees, the Act proposed will not become a standing law of the Church. This Act with some amendments and additions, but without substantial change, has remained continuously in force even to the present time.

When negotiations for the Union of the Parliaments began to take shape, the Church was naturally alarmed. In a British Parliament, where members of the Church of England would be in an overwhelming majority, and in whose Upper House the Anglican Bishops would sit, what possible security could Scotland have that her National Church would not be tampered with? At length an arrangement was made which holds to this day, and which had the effect of removing the hitherto insuperable objections of the Church of Scotland. An Act for the maintenance of the Presbyterian Church of Scotland was passed and inserted in the Act ratifying the treaty of Union (1707), and it was provided that each British Sovereign should, immediately on accession, and before his coronation, take an oath to maintain "the government, worship, discipline, rights and privileges of the Church of Scotland." The signing of this oath is the first official act of the sovereign, and on it depends his claim to the allegiance of Scotsmen.

CHAPTER VII

THE EIGHTEENTH CENTURY

WITH the Revolution Settlement the constitutional development of Scottish Presbyterianism reached its maturity ; and with the Treaty of Union the arrangement then made became part of the British Constitution. The remainder of its history may therefore be traced in briefer outline. It will be largely a record of schism and the healing of schism ; and it is characteristic that the cause of that schism has been neither doctrine nor administration, but the assertion of the rights of the people and of the Church as against the patron and the State. The great dissenting bodies of Scotland have not only remained Presbyterian, but have founded themselves on the claim to represent the original principles of the Church of Scotland more faithfully even than the Establishment which they left, or which cast them out. They did not strive for novel views, but for ancient positions, and this was one secret of their growth; they called for no unsettlement of the religious convictions or instincts of their people, but only for an intensification of elements which were already there. It is from this fact that there comes the possibility of re-union without parting with ancient tradition or the sacrifice of ancient principles.

The earlier years of the eighteenth century saw the Church of Scotland taking effective possession of the whole land, making special efforts to bring the Gaelic-speaking districts, where there had apparently been a revival of Romanism, within the Church's sway, and filling up parishes vacated by the death of Episcopal ministers with those who loyally accepted the Presbyterian system. Its efforts were successful. A few glens and islands still remained faithful to Rome, and in some districts a number of congregations ministered to by the non-juring Episcopal clergy continued to exist. But more and more the mass of the people not only acquiesced in the Established Church but became staunch adherents to its principles alike against Romanism and against the Scottish Episcopal Church.

The fortunes of that Church, as now constituted apart from the Church of Scotland, demand a brief notice. Gaining toleration at first from a sympathetic Parliament in London, it was again put under severe restrictions when the rising of 1715 showed it to be absolutely Jacobite in sympathy. After 1745 it was still more rigidly repressed, and seemed on the point of extinction. The support it at first obtained from the Church of England, and from the Englishmen who came to reside permanently or temporarily in Scotland, was more than neutralized by the disfavour of Government, which looked upon it—with good grounds—as in league with the banished Stewart dynasty. Feuds distracted the clergy; bishops were consecrated against bishops. Even the Church of England ceased to favour it as non-juring, and Anglican congregations were formed in Scotland; the Church of England was now staunchly Hanoverian. But undoubtedly persecution and spiritual freedom helped to refine and chasten Scottish Episcopacy; it became more the Church of Leighton and less the Church of Sharp. Meantime it drew away from its old forms of worship, from doctrinal standards and other traditions which it had held in common with Scottish Presbyterianism. It early accepted the English Book of Common Prayer; it even took up a "higher" position than the Church of England in doctrine and in ritual, and embodied the difference in its Communion office. At last the death of Charles Edward Stewart in 1788 left the Episcopal clergy free to transfer their allegiance to the House of Hanover and to pray for George III. Parliament responded to their new loyalty, and, with the goodwill of the Church of Scotland, removed their legal disabilities (1792). Still "a shadow of a shade" as regards popular support up to the end of the century, the Scottish Episcopal Church had a considerable number of adherents among the nobility and gentry. It was as time went on both modified and strengthened by the influence of the Anglican Church, especially on Scotsmen whose education or business led them for a time to reside in England. The Thirty-nine Articles were adopted in 1804 as the doctrinal standard of the Scottish Episcopal Church.

At the other pole of difference from the Church as Established, the Cameronians continued to protest vigorously against the defections in Church and State from covenanting principles and obligations, and they claimed as stoutly as the Episcopal clergy to be the true Church in an apostate land. They were but a small and scattered handful, chiefly found in the south-west of Scotland, and a grievous thorn there in the side of the Establishment. Two or three ministers joined them, so that in 1743 they were able to form a "Reformed Presbytery," and somewhat to extend their influence.

Meantime the Church went on its way, supplying ordinances to the whole country, administering discipline, fostering education, and maintaining with little change the form of worship which it had adopted in the middle of the previous century. But a bone of contention was early cast in its midst. An Act of Parliament, obtained mainly by the efforts of Jacobites avowed and secret, had been passed in the year 1712, restoring patronage of Church livings to the ancient patrons. The bill was introduced into the House of Commons on the 13th of March and passed so rapidly that by April 7th it had gone through all its stages in that House and was brought up to the House of Lords on the following day. The Church of Scotland had taken alarm and had sent representatives to London to protest, but they were too late to obtain justice. They were heard by counsel before the House of Lords, but that House passed the second and third readings of the Bill on the same day, and by April 14th it had been returned to the Commons with some trifling amendments, and ultimately received the Royal Assent on the 22nd, about forty days after it first saw the light. It is worth recording that of the thirteen Bishops who were present, five voted against the Bill. Other measures favouring Episcopal ministers were passed about the same time; and, as every student of history knows, there was considerable danger of a Jacobite triumph in these last years of Queen Anne. But George I came to the throne; and the rising of 1715 was crushed.

The Patronage Act, however, in spite of the

protests of the Church, was not repealed. It was a grievous wrong to Scotland and its Church. It was a violation not only of the spirit of the Treaty of Union, but even, on a fair interpretation, of its letter. It made a fundamental change in the mode of appointing ministers, because it supplanted the local heritors and elders, who knew and represented the people, and that in favour of a patron who might be, and often was, non-resident and absolutely out of sympathy with them. The system it superseded may have been defective in its working; but it was capable of amendment, and it might have been so reformed that the cherished rights of the people to have no minister "intruded" upon them could have been combined with the preliminary presentation of a qualified candidate by men of weight and standing in the parish and its congregation.

Scotland has lost as well as gained by the Union with England ; one of its greatest losses was the Patronage Act with the evils it wrought in the next century and a half.

The Act of 1712 was not greatly taken advantage of at first; the circumstances of its origin discredited it, and for more than seventy years the Church never ceased to protest against it. But it remained upon the statute book, and patrons gradually began to make presentations. The Church endeavoured to pledge its ministers and licentiates against receiving such presentations, and to maintain the principle embodied in the Revolution Settlement, that the heritors and elders should present, and the people approve or "call" the minister, the presbytery to be judge of the case should the people disapprove. But some of the ministers and people went further. Falling back on the First and Second Books of Discipline, and on the legislation of 1649 regarding the election of ministers, they claimed on Covenanting grounds that the call from the people was the essential thing. Thus when, in 1732, the Assembly passed an Act requiring presbyteries, in cases where a patron had not made a presentation, to proceed to induct a minister upon a "call" from the heritors (being Protestants) and the elders, a violent opposition arose, led by Ebenezer Erskine. Erskine was a man of ancient lineage and great earnestness of character ; a combination which has always appealed to the Scottish nation. He and three other ministers protested against the procedure of the Assembly, and on their refusal to retract the protest were declared on account of their contumacy to be no longer ministers of the Church of Scotland. They found sympathisers, lay and clerical, in many parts of the country, and they proceeded to form a presbytery— the Associate Presbytery—and so the first organized secession was launched. Alarmed at the result, the Church in the General Assembly of 1734 endeavoured

to retrace its steps and recall the seceders, even by
rescinding the Act of 1732. It was in vain ; they
refused to be reponed ; and after endeavouring for
seven years to bring them to a conciliatory frame
of mind, during which time they were allowed to
remain in possession of their parishes, the Church
deposed them in 1740.

The truth is that the seceders represented a body
of opinion in the Church which was really Covenanting alike in name and in spirit, and which was
uneasy at many of the developments of the preceding
forty years. Patronage, or its abuse, was by no means
their only grievance against the majority in the Church.
In their "Judicial Testimony" of 1736, among other
enormities against which they lifted up their witness, they included the non-renewal of the Covenant
at the Revolution, the permission of Episcopal
ministers to remain in their parishes, the union with
England on a non-covenanting basis, the resultant
toleration, the slackness of the Church in dealing
with heresy, and even the abolition of the penal
statutes against witches in defiance of the law of God
which says, "Thou shalt not suffer a witch to live."
In these seceders dwelt the intense, passionate and
narrow spirit of the Protesters of 1651. Earnest,
devout and spiritual as they were, they were looking
backward and not forward, and felt easier when they
found themselves outside an Establishment which

was yielding to forward movements. Yet their manly independence, their personal character, their active piety and their self-sacrificing efforts in maintaining an educated ministry have contributed factors of the highest value to the development of Scottish religious life.

Mention having been made of heresy, it should be said that while the Church was at this period very sensitive to any alleged defections from doctrinal orthodoxy in the preaching of its ministers, the General Assembly, as a rule, dealt patiently and considerately with those who were brought to its bar on the charge.

The Seceders' arrows searched every joint in the armour of the Church, but they often rebounded, and the diverse attitude of religious parties after the Secession was illustrated on the occasion of Whitfield's visits to Scotland. He came in 1741 at the invitation of the Seceders. But he would not sign the Solemn League and Covenant or promise to confine his preaching to the Seceders. So they parted. Whitfield preached in parish churches and in the open air. Great excitement followed. Independently an extraordinary revival of religion broke out at Cambuslang, and Whitfield returned to join in the movement. Seceders and Cameronians denounced it as a work of the devil. No good thing could come from a "prelatic hireling" like Whitfield.

Strife was hushed for a little by the rising of
1745. Ebenezer Erskine personally took up arms
against the rebels ; and the Church and the Secession
both stood stoutly for the Hanoverian dynasty and
the Protestant Succession. Presently the Seceders
had troubles of their own. The more extreme spirits
to whom "every pin of the tabernacle was precious,"
and who spent much energy in looking for "pins,"
discovered that the Burgess Oath which exacted
acceptance of "the true religion presently professed
within these realms and authorized by the laws
thereof," was inconsistent with the Covenant and the
Secession testimony. After furious internal strife,
the Anti-burghers, as they came to be called, actually
excommunicated the Burghers, including Ebenezer
Erskine and his brother Ralph ! Thus from 1747
there were two bodies of Seceders, each claiming to
be the inheritors of the true principles of the Reformation. But the Church did not profit by these
divisions, for the number of disputed settlements of
ministers continued great, and many a settlement
made against popular feeling gave rise to a local
secession and the founding of a new congregation,
Burgher or Anti-burgher. There was no definite rule
of procedure, and, in cases of dispute, sometimes the
patron's presentee, sometimes the heritors' and elders'
nominee, and sometimes the man called by the people
was settled in the charge by the General Assembly.

There was usually great unwillingness to coerce presbyteries and so to create further secessions ; and the General Assembly, when it found itself compelled to induct a presentee against the wishes of the people and the local presbytery, usually did so by a "riding committee" of its own, which discharged the duty the presbytery were unwilling to discharge. This procedure not only increased the confusion and ill-feeling prevalent throughout the Church, but was really an evasion of the principles of Presbyterian Church government. The confusion was ended for a time by the formation and rise to ascendancy of the "Moderate" party.

The Moderates were the party of culture and order as opposed to the more enthusiastic and fervent preachers whom they called the High-flyers ; their preaching dwelt upon moral duties and graces rather than upon doctrines ; they were eager to bring the Church into closer alliance with art and literature ; and they repudiated the extreme Puritanic strictness of conduct which had long marked the Scottish clergy. They considered that a patron, himself a man of position and education, would be more likely to select one whose culture, education and training would fit him for the high office to which he was to be called, than would be the case if the choice were left to the congregation at large. They insisted therefore that the parliamentary law should be obeyed, that the presentees of patrons should be accepted by the presbyteries after satisfaction given as to life, learning, and doctrine only, that the call of the people was immaterial, and that presbyteries should be compelled by the General Assembly to do their duty in inducting qualified presentees. After 1752 the Moderates began to acquire an ascendancy in the Church ; and in a generation it was complete. Unflinching advocates of law and order in everything, they brought the procedure of the General Assembly to an admirable pitch of consistency and regularity ; and presbyterial machinery at length moved smoothly and easily. At no period, moreover, were the clergy of the Church more closely in touch with the literary movements of the age than under the ascendancy of the Moderates, with Principal Robertson, the eminent historian, at their head.

But they bought peace and order at a great price. Patrons became careless and indifferent, and the patronage of the Crown was often used for political purposes. Every unpopular settlement strengthened the Secession. Thomas Gillespie, minister of Carnock, was deposed in 1752, by way of example, being the most prominent member of the recalcitrant presbytery of Dunfermline, which had refused to induct a minister to whom the congregation were strongly opposed. Gillespie had a church built for him by

his sympathizers in that town, and in 1761, finding
two other ministers holding similar views with himself, he formed with them the Presbytery of Relief.
The name indicated their desire to remain on
friendly terms with the Establishment and to afford
in their churches relief to its members who might be
oppressed by the operation of patronage. A genuine
liberality and charity towards others who could not
see eye to eye with them marked the Relief Church.
They were of another spirit from the first Seceders—
the Associate Presbytery. Nevertheless, they were
seceders, and as their tolerant attitude was not
reciprocated by the Church of Scotland, the gulf
between it and them inevitably widened.

Alarmed and ashamed at the progress of dissent,
the Popular party, as it was called in opposition to
the Moderate party in the Church, endeavoured to
shake off or to mitigate the yoke of Patronage. By
1773, one hundred and eighty congregations of the
Secession or Relief bodies had been formed ; the
origin of which could in nearly every case be traced
to the Act of 1712. The Church might well feel
alarmed. But Moderatism was then too strong to be
overcome, and the struggle ended for the time when
in 1784 the General Assembly struck out from the
directions annually given to its Commission the
clause, long merely formal, instructing it to seize any
convenient season that might occur to petition for

the redress of the grievance caused by the Act of 1712.

The closing years of the century saw Moderatism supreme in the Church, but altered for the worse alike in its character and its influence. It had been found that patrons, when altogether freed from the necessity of consulting the wishes and spiritual needs of the people, were far from being universally anxious to discover men of character, learning and ability to place in the parishes in their gift. Their choice of a minister often fell upon the candidate most subservient or most useful to themselves. The nominee of the laird or (in Crown livings) of the Government was no better qualified in intellectual attainments than the people's favourite, and often fell short of him in moral and religious earnestness. The Church, as a whole, was lacking in religious fervour, and refused to launch out on the new tide of religious life which was beginning to rise around it. Proposals to enter upon missions to the heathen were not accepted; the pulpits were closed to all but ministers and licentiates of the Establishment. The dread of the French Revolution helped to strengthen resistance to new enterprises, while it failed to resuscitate ancient zeal and piety.

The majority of the Seceders also were still stiffly conservative in matters of religion and, though they retained their characteristic earnestness, they were more concerned with the minutiae of their peculiar doctrines than with the great movements of the human spirit which were beginning to agitate the world. A new controversy regarding the province of the civil magistrate arose both among the Burghers and the Anti-burghers, and again they both split into sections, the former in 1799, the latter in 1806. Thus in the early years of the nineteenth century there were many and various schools of those who dissented from the Church of Scotland, viz. the Episcopalians and Cameronians (or "Reformed Presbyterians"), whose separation dated from the Revolution, four branches of the Secession of 1740, and the Relief Church, dating from 1761. Congregationalists, Baptists, Wesleyans, and some minute sects had also found an open lodgment in Scotland during the preceding century. The Church of Scotland, however, retained an undoubted predominance.

The discipline of the Church during the century had abated in its rigour. Successive statutes had removed civil consequences from excommunication and other ecclesiastical sentences, and limited the jurisdiction of the Church to those who were members of it. Even in regard to these there was a certain mitigation of penalties in practice. But public confession, rebuke, and restoration were still practised; fines even were still inflicted for moral offences. Social, if not civil, coercion was

a potent instrument in the Church's hand for enforcing obedience to its moral and ecclesiastical code.
But a sense of failure to touch the real springs of
moral evil by the public exposure of sin was beginning to be widely felt.

Public worship seems to have become generally
impoverished by the abandonment of the regular
reading of the Scriptures.   On the other hand, the
praise of the Church was enriched by the addition to
the metrical Psalter of "Paraphrases" of selected
portions of the Scriptures.   In many quarters the
great gatherings of ministers and people at the infrequent "Sacrament" seasons were a most prominent
feature of the religious life of the country, but these
were often sadly marred by the inevitable evils
connected with the concourse of crowds of whose
assemblage piety was not the sole cause.

CHAPTER VIII

Revival and Conflict

THE earlier years of the nineteenth century were marked by the growth in numbers and influence of the Evangelical party. They carried on the traditional devoutness and energy of the Popular party and its championship of the people's rights, but they exhibited also a new liberality and intellectual vigour.

During the latter half of the eighteenth century the antagonism between Moderates and Evangelicals had dominated Church politics; nearly half a century more was to run before their opposition became so bitter that actual separation became more tolerable than internal strife. Yet too much may be made of their differences; these were not fundamental. They must be attributed rather to temperament and to policy than to deep-seated principle.

At the extremity of the Moderate wing might be found men careless as to vital religion, and content to perform ecclesiastical duties in a perfunctory way, mere "stipend-lifters"; at the extremity of the other might be found simple fanatics for doctrinal ortho- doxy, zealous for Evangelical faith to the verge of antinomianism. Some regarded the Church as little more than a department of State; some would claim for it independent powers for which the Pope might sigh. But there were always middle men, whom cir- cumstances, rather than deliberate choice, labelled with a party name. And until a momentous crisis raised men's feeling to fever heat, even the leaders of the parties remained on a friendly footing, and could work together for great causes. Principal Robertson and Dr John Erskine, the trusted chiefs of the two schools in earlier days, were collegiate ministers of Old Greyfriars Church, Edinburgh, and lived in harmony; indeed, on the death of the former, his colleague preached a very noble and appreciative funeral sermon. In later days, leading men on both sides united in the movement for Roman Catholic emancipation and in the organization of Foreign Missions under the direct management of the Church. Human nature being what it is, the harmonious fusion of intense religious earnestness with intellec- tual liberality will always be difficult, and there will remain the danger of conflicting parties being formed, one tainted with fanaticism and the other with scep- ticism. Yet had Scotland been free to shape its own

policy, more particularly in the matter of ecclesiastical
patronage, there seems little reason to doubt that the
undivided Church could have continued to use, for
its one supreme aim, the combined gifts and energies
of all its leading men.

The whole Church was bracing itself up for the
fuller discharge of its responsibilities. In 1810 Parliament voted £10,000 annually to augment the stipends of the most poorly endowed parishes; and later
on built and meagrely endowed forty churches in
destitute districts of the Highlands. The Church
responded by increasing its own efforts. Chapels
of ease were erected in growing towns and in manufacturing and mining villages; and the religious needs
of a rapidly increasing population received increasing
attention. Missionary Societies had been founded in
Edinburgh and Glasgow, and were working abroad.
Now by a movement inclusive of both parties in the
Church, missions to the heathen world, under the
direction of a Committee of the General Assembly,
were begun by the dispatch of Alexander Duff to
India in the year 1829 as the first accredited missionary of the Church.

The Seceders had by this time mostly become
opponents of Church Establishments, and were a
formidable body to reckon with. The stage of their
existence devoted to quarrelling among themselves
had passed away. Finding themselves flourishing on

the support of their own people, and peculiarly open
to the democratic ideas then prevalent, most of them
had adopted Voluntary principles, abjured extreme
Covenanting tenets, and were beginning to draw
together again.   In 1820 the principal bodies of
Burghers and Anti-burghers coalesced under the
name of the United Secession. They speedily showed
themselves an earnest and active Church, intellectu-
ally and religiously alive, and they became advocates
of the disestablishment of the Church on the ground
of principle.   The union of Church and State, hitherto practically unchallenged in Scotland, was now for
the first time made an object of criticism and of
attack.

None of their assaults upon the constitution and
life of the Church of Scotland was felt so keenly as
that which they made upon the law of Patronage
and its results.   The Evangelical party had never
ceased to maintain the rights of the people in the
choice of their minister, and even many who were in
the ranks of the Moderates were desirous of seeing
more power exercised by the presbyteries in rejecting
presentees whom they knew to be unacceptable and
therefore unprofitable to the people.   Moreover, the
increasing interest and zeal of the people in the work
of the Church naturally strengthened their claim for
a greater voice in the appointment of their own
ministers.   The year 1834 witnessed the beginning

of a struggle, chiefly over the question of Patronage, known in Scottish ecclesiastical annals as the Ten Years' Conflict, which ended in a secession so unparalleled in its magnitude and importance as to win for it the name of the "Disruption."

Since the year 1752 the General Assembly, by a series of decisions, had limited the powers of the presbytery to a trial of the life, learning and doctrine of the patron's presentee, and treated as immaterial the objections of the people, or the slenderness of the "call." It was now proposed to authorize presbyteries to give weight to the objections of the people. The Moderate party were willing to go so far. But in 1834 the General Assembly went further, and passed an Act declaring it to be a fundamental law of the Church that no pastor should be intruded on any congregation contrary to the will of the people, and instructing presbyteries to reject any presentee of whom the majority of male heads of families disapproved. The minority in the Assembly expressed doubts of the compatibility of this "Veto Act" with the statute law, especially the Act of 1712, and objected to the disapproval of a bare majority of male heads of families being made an absolute bar to the collation of the presentee. The law officers of the Crown and some eminent counsel also, had, however, held that the Veto Act was in accordance with statute law.

Another important Act known as the Chapel Act was passed by the same Assembly. Very largely by the inspiring eloquence and personal influence of Dr Thomas Chalmers, Church extension had made great progress. Two hundred chapels of ease had been built and supplied with ministers. But these not being parish ministers had no seats in the courts of the Church. It was resolved by the "Chapel Act" to assign districts to these churches as parishes *quoad sacra*, to give them Kirk Sessions, and to put their ministers upon the same level as others in powers and privileges. It was claimed that this could be done in virtue of the Church's sole jurisdiction and inherent freedom in spiritual matters. But a strong minority considered legislative enactment by the civil authorities as also necessary, and leading men even among the Evangelicals disapproved of the Chapel Act.

As anticipated by many, a conflict soon arose with the civil courts. Patrons and presentees appealed to the Court of Session, the Supreme Court in Scotland, against decisions of presbyteries made in accordance with the Veto Act. And in 1838 that court decided in what was called the Auchterarder case, that a presbytery had no right to reject a presentee on the sole ground of objection by a majority of male heads of families. The decision of the Court of Session was only made by a majority of eight as against a minority of five judges; so that the action taken by the Church cannot be regarded as having been manifestly illegal from the first. The law, however, was now declared. The Veto Act was found contrary to statute law. The question was: What would the Church do? Dr Chalmers himself, in a well-known pamphlet written some time after the Assembly of 1840, said the Veto Act would not have been enacted had they foreseen the decision of the Civil Courts that they had made an infringement of civil rights. He adds, as might be expected, that while they would not have given up the principle of non-intrusion, "they would have devised some other method for carrying the principle into operation." Dr Chalmers makes it clear that even in that year, if it would have brought peace, he would have been in favour of the Assembly rescinding the Act, and he adds, "We make no surrender of our spiritual independence by giving up the Veto Law when done by our own act; neither do we propose to surrender the cause of non-intrusion. We only surrender one of the expedients by which we had hoped to have provided for it," and further on in the same pamphlet he wrote, "the first thing which, in our estimation, the Church ought to do, is to repeal the Veto Law."

The dominant majority in the General Assembly would not consent to anything which could be interpreted as submission to the Civil Courts. During

the years between 1834 and 1838 the Church had
been growing in zeal and activity, and in determination to maintain its spiritual independence, as understood and interpreted by the more extreme of its
members. Religious enthusiasm and a revival of the
covenanting spirit grew upon ministers and laymen
of the Evangelical party. They determined to resist
what they considered and called an encroachment
upon the Crown rights of the Redeemer, the Lord
Jesus Christ, the only Head of the Church. The
General Assembly of 1838 made a strong Declaration
of Spiritual Independence, and of their determination
to enforce obedience to their Acts upon all the office-
bearers and members of the Church. As showing
the truth of the statement that it was no point of
fundamental principle which really divided the con-
tending parties in the Church, it is worth noting
that in moving this Declaration of Independence,
Dr Buchanan relied on and quoted the speeches of
two leaders of the Moderate party. He did this to
prove how completely they supported the doctrine
of the Spiritual Independence of the Church and
condemned the view of the Court of Session that by
alliance with the State the Church had lost the rights
and powers inherent in its Constitution. If it is
necessary to add further testimony on this point,
reference may be made to Dr Hanna (the son-in-law
of Chalmers) who writing in 1861 said, "The contro-

versy between us and the Established Church does not touch the doctrine of Christ's Headship as taught in Holy Writ so as to give any grounds for saying that we uphold, and the Established Church denies that Headship."

Meanwhile the Auchterarder case had been appealed to the House of Lords. The House of Lords unanimously dismissed the appeal, and in their opinions declared the presbytery restricted to try only the life, learning and doctrine of a presentee. In fact, they judicially tied the Church down to the older Moderate position, and denied any rights to the people at all. These sweeping opinions, by making it impossible for the Church to withdraw the Veto Act and to fall back simply upon the discretion of presbyteries, which many had hitherto considered ample enough to safeguard the people's interest, provoked still more resolute resistance from the Assembly of 1839. It was resolved that the emoluments of the parish should henceforth, in obedience to the civil law, go unchallenged to the patron's nominee. But to the spiritual office he could not be admitted, unless in accordance with the Church's law. Unfortunately, however, he could not draw the emoluments until he was invested with the spiritual office, so that the concession made by the Church to the civil power was inoperative. A Committee to consider the situation, and confer, if necessary, with the Government, was appointed.

It was undoubtedly a case for conference. Had
the Government been a strong one, or even had it
appreciated the gravity of the situation, it could have
satisfied by legislation the requirements of the Church,
without essential alteration in the terms of the alliance between Church and State. The Whig Government, then tottering to its fall, would do nothing;
the Conservative opposition was thought to be more
favourable. But a more critical situation now developed. The presbytery of Strathbogie bowed to
the authority of the Court of Session, disregarded
that of the Assembly, and agreed to take on trial
a presentee who had been "vetoed" by the congregation. The seven members of the presbytery who
had carried this were suspended by the Church, so
that their presbyterial functions devolved upon the
minority of four. But the majority continued to discharge their functions, both in their parishes and as
a presbytery, and the scandal was presented of two
rival presbyteries in the same district at open strife,
one recognized by the civil judicature and the other
by the ecclesiastical. The dominant party in the
Church grew more determined than ever. They
had now some hopes of obtaining parliamentary
recognition of their claims. The Duke of Argyll
brought in a Bill, which would have substantially
legalized the Veto Act; it obtained the approval of
the Assembly of 1841, but it was swept away by the

dissolution of Parliament, which occurred in that year.

The same Assembly deposed the Strathbogie majority. Yet they continued to officiate, and their friends throughout the country recognized and aided them. The breach between the parties was growing irreparable. A final offer by the Conservative Government of a Bill, which came nearly to the limits of the Veto Act, but left more power of discretion to the presbytery, was accepted and then rejected by the Non-intrusion Committee of the Assembly. In the following Assembly (1842), a resolution was carried that Patronage was contrary to Scripture, and ought to be abolished. A Claim of Right was passed, in which the independent spiritual jurisdiction of the Church was theologically and historically defined and vindicated, and recent proceedings of the State condemned as unlawful and unconstitutional. A few Evangelicals showed some uneasiness at the rejection of the Government's proposed measure, but the majority went on in their course. For receiving the Lord's Supper at the hands of the deposed Strathbogie ministers, eleven leading men among the Moderates were suspended from judicial functions for nine months.

The strife of jurisdictions grew more scandalous and complicated every month. At last, on appeal, the House of Lords decided that the members of a presbytery refusing to induct a qualified presentee were liable to pay damages for the pecuniary loss inflicted on him. The situation as now developed could not last, and a great meeting of Evangelical ministers determined to make a final representation to Government, and, if that should be unsuccessful, to secede. Their resolution was deepened by another decision of the Court of Session, which pronounced it unlawful for the General Assembly to admit chapel ministers to the status of parish ministers. This decision not only nullified the Chapel Act of 1834, but cast a shadow of illegality on all the proceedings subsequent to that date of all courts in which chapel ministers had sat as members. Thus both the great Acts of 1834 were now declared by the civil judicature to have been passed incompetently.

The Government declined to go further than they had already offered to go, and insisted that the Church should recognize the decisions of the civil courts. A motion was then made in the House of Commons for an enquiry into the grievances of the Church. The great majority of the Scottish members supported it, but an overwhelming combination of English members of both parties threw it out. The Non-intrusionists now prepared for secession, and great sums of money were raised both for building churches and for maintaining the ministry.

The General Assembly met on the 18th of May, 1843. According to custom, the retiring Moderator,

when the members had assembled after the usual
sermon in St Giles's Church, opened the meeting with
prayer; but instead of proceeding with the usual
business, he read a forcible protest against the recent
acts of the civil power as contrary to the terms of the
union between Church and State, bowed to the Lord
High Commissioner, and left the place of meeting,
followed by the bulk of the ministers and elders of
the Evangelical party. The seceders walked in pro-
cession to a hall which had been prepared to receive
them, and there formed themselves into the Free
Church of Scotland. The Church of Scotland had
suffered the long-threatened Disruption.

With marvellous energy and magnificent devotion
the Free Church not only established itself in every
corner of the land, but also continued to maintain
the missionary schemes which the undivided Church
had carried on. Claiming to be the true Church of
Scotland, the Free Church entered upon a splendid
career of evangelistic and pastoral activity, with a
determination also to maintain the highest standard
of equipment for its ministry. The "Sustentation
Fund," as it was called, enlisted the regular contribution, great or small, of every member for the support
of the ministry throughout the country; and the
Church stood forth as a noble example of a self-
sustaining, energetic, and compact organization,
endeavouring to face national responsibilities on

the highest Presbyterian principles. The one blot on its escutcheon was the malignant vituperation with which many of its ministers and members assailed their brethren who remained in the Establishment, combined with the assumption of a spiritual superiority for the Free Church.

The Church of Scotland lay a seeming wreck. It is true that, after all, only 451 ministers seceded and 752 remained. When it came to the point of secession, many who had been members of the dominant Evangelical party held back, some because they did not yet despair of winning constitutionally from the State recognition of the just claims of the National Church, some because they felt they had gone too far in defiance of the civil authority, and some perhaps because of the greatness of the sacrifice demanded from them. Of the Moderates also it should be said that among them some of the finest and noblest spirits of the Church were to be found, such as James Robertson and Norman Macleod, men at once evangelical and moderate in no party sense. Yet it cannot be denied that the majority of the most zealous and active among both clergy and laity left the Church in 1843.

CHAPTER IX

Development and Re-union

WHEN the lapse of a few years permitted men calmly to gauge the situation, it was found that the Church of Scotland, though sadly diminished in strength, was not moribund as its enemies believed it to be. Under able leadership, it began to rally in the very shock of the Disruption. In 1843 Parliament passed a Benefices Act, which entitled Presbyteries to take into consideration the objections of the people to presentees. In 1844 another Act was passed enabling the Church to set up new parishes *quoad sacra*, which had been the object of the Chapel Act of 1834. Endowments for such parishes began to come in from voluntary subscriptions. Missionary activity was resumed, and the Church received from its members an increasing amount of pecuniary support for all enterprises at home and abroad. Churches which had been emptied were again filled, and in a

few years it became apparent that outside some of
the Highland counties the affections of the people
remained to a large extent with the Church of Scotland and the principles for which it stood.

A movement for the complete repeal of the Act
of 1712 was inaugurated about the year 1866. Those
who moved for the abolition of Patronage did so on
two grounds. Historically, it was a grievance which
had been the cause of much evil, while beyond all
doubt, some of the leaders hoped that it would be
regarded as one at least of the preliminary steps
towards union, or co-operation. Ultimately the
movement was successful; in 1874 an Act of Parliament was passed repealing the Act of 1712, and vest-
ing the right of election to benefices in the regular
communicants, along with such adherents as the
Church, through its own courts, might decide to
admit to the roll in each parish. The hopes entertained that this measure might lead to re-union with
the Free Church, the Church's demands in 1834—43
having now, to a very large extent, been met by
legislative enactment, were not realized. Instead of
that result, a movement for the disestablishment
and disendowment of the Church of Scotland was
inaugurated.

While quitting what they deemed to be a vitiated
Establishment the Free Churchmen had still cherished
the principle of a National Church, and would gladly

have returned to alliance with the State on the
acceptance of their own terms as to spiritual independence. They were not Voluntaries. But as years
went on, they began to realize the hopelessness of
such a restoration, and they and the older seceders
naturally drew nearer to one another. As we have
seen, the eighteenth century had been fertile in
secessions and schisms. There were schisms, and
schisms from schisms, Seceders and Relief, Burghers
and Anti-burghers, Old Lights and New Lights. So
little did separation from the State make for unity.
We have also seen that a better spirit began to
manifest itself in the early decades of the nineteenth
century, and that, in 1820, a really considerable
number of those who had seceded came together
under the name of the United Secession Church. In
1847, there was a further coalition with the Relief
Church and the name United Presbyterian Church
was adopted.

The United Presbyterians, as a body, were opposed
to the alliance of Church and State. The Free Churchmen, while maintaining that principle, were dissatis-
fied with the Establishment from which they had
seceded. Their attitude was difficult to maintain or
to justify, and there was a gradual trend towards
closer relations with the United Presbyterians, and
also towards the adoption of an attitude of hostility
to the continuance of the existing relation between

Church and State. Negotiations for union between
these Churches were begun, but so strong a resistance was made by a powerful minority in the Free
Church on the principle of the national recognition
of religion, securely embedded in the constitution
and standards of the Free Church, that the proposed
union was in 1872 indefinitely postponed.

Nor was the destructive side of the movement
more successful than the constructive. The agitation
for the disestablishment and disendowment of the
Church never commanded much popular sympathy
in Scotland, and the force of the movement soon
passed away.

The Church of Scotland had never ceased to
desire or work for the re-union of Scottish Presbyterianism. That desire found expression in com-
munications which took place between the Churches
in 1878 and 1879. In 1878 the Church of Scotland
issued an invitation "to frank and friendly conference," accompanied with a declaration of willingness
to take any steps towards co-operation and union
"consistent with the maintenance and support of an
establishment of religion" and "the sacredness of
the ancient endowments." The United Presbyterian
Church replied in 1879 that while they regarded
it as impossible for them to share the trust reposed
in the Church of Scotland, they agreed to "co-
operation" at home, and especially abroad, and

expressed a desire for the institution of a regular channel of communication between the Churches. The Free Church sent a reply which was equally friendly in tone, and said that it agreed " to maintain inviolate the principle of a national recognition of religion in accordance with the Confession of Faith." It went on to make a reference to the documents of 1842 and 1843, and advanced a claim to be regarded as the true representative of the Church of Scotland, adding that these documents contained the only principle upon which the Churches would ever be re-united. Political agitation did not prevent the Church of Scotland in 1886 from renewing its invitation to conference, but again its overtures led to no practical result.

It is true, however, to say that all through this period the wisest and most far-seeing men in all the Churches, while aware that re-union could not be attained without a strong public opinion in its favour and that it could not, with advantage, be pressed further at the time, were, in the words of Lord Gordon, who as Lord Advocate was largely responsible for the Act of 1874, "looking forward to the prospect of a successful attempt to effect the re-union of the Scottish Presbyterian forces."

The history of the re-union of the non-established Scottish Presbyterian Churches may at this point be concluded. The Free Church was joined in 1876 by

the bulk of the Reformed Presbyterians or Cameronians. And after a quarter of a century, the
negotiations with the United Presbyterian Church
were resumed, and in 1900 the Free Church and the
United Presbyterian Church became one, under the
name of the United Free Church.

The Free Church had had experience since 1843
that, though it "went out" to secure its spiritual
independence from the interference of the civil courts,
these courts never hesitated to adjudge any case
brought by a minister or member alleging breach
of contract against the Church; and in 1900 it took
a great risk as a Church which had hitherto maintained the "establishment principle," in uniting with
a confessedly voluntary body. Some thirty of its
ministers and a certain proportion of the members
refused to enter the Union. Cross-actions were
brought between the uniting majority and the dis-
sentient minority, each seeking to be declared the
rightful holder in trust of the Free Church property.
The Scottish Courts decided in favour of the former;
but on appeal the House of Lords, by a majority, decided
in favour of the latter (1904). By passing a certain
Declaratory Act in which, it was held, the doctrine
of the Confession had been modified, and by ceasing
to maintain the principle of an Established Church,
the majority, it was declared, had ceased to represent
the Free Church. The ministers and their people

who held by the ancient standards unmodified were
declared to be the Free Church of Scotland, and
entitled to hold its eleven hundred churches and all its
property, at home and abroad. As they were manifestly unable to discharge their trust, Parliament
was called upon to set matters right by legislation.
This was done by the Scottish Churches Act of 1905.
A Parliamentary Commission was appointed to allot
the property so that the purpose of the trust should
be fulfilled; and, in consequence, the greater part,
including most of the churches, was restored to the
majority, now comprehended in the United Free
Church.

The essential justice of this action by Parliament
is generally admitted, and by none more heartily
than by the Church of Scotland. At the same time,
the case has shown how vain it is to expect that
a Church which holds property, gathers funds, and
has a settled constitution can keep such matters out
of the civil courts, if in any of its acts it may be
held to infringe the rights of a minority or of an
individual.

During these years of strangely mingled rivalry
and fraternity the Churches have been individually
facing their religious responsibilities with an ever-
growing sense of their greatness. At the Union of 1707
the population of Scotland was still under a million,
and the parish churches numbered about 920. The

people of Scotland now number nearly five millions. But it is not enough to take account only of the growth of the population. Its centre of gravity has so to speak shifted. While the agricultural districts have diminished, the cities and towns have enormously increased in population; mining and manufacturing communities have been formed and are still springing up.

Not only, therefore, has the need of provision for the religious wants of the people grown, but a new principle of distribution has been required. Noble efforts have been made to keep pace with the growing needs, but each Church having to provide in the first place for its own people, it has not been found possible to take a sufficiently comprehensive survey of the whole problem by one authority, and a certain amount of competition has been the result. The villages, as a rule, are over-churched; the great mining and manufacturing districts are under-churched.

After the passage of the Act of 1844, already mentioned, the old Church Accommodation Committee of the Church of Scotland, which had built 200 additional churches, became known as the Home Mission Committee, and the Endowment Committee was formed. Since that time these two Committees have worked in close co-operation; the Home Mission Committee, in the first instance, aiding the building of new churches, and the temporary support of the ministry in them; and the Endowment Committee supplying one half, and local effort the other half, of the sum necessary to secure a permanent endowment of at least £120 a year, which is meant to be the nucleus of ministerial income. In recent years the demands have not been so urgent, but the work of endowing new churches is going on at the rate of five every year. The total number of parishes thus endowed by voluntary effort has now reached 460, and these have been endowed at a cost of something like one and three quarter million sterling.

The old parishes, including those sanctioned in 1824 by Parliament for the Highlands and Islands, are less than one thousand in number, but with the *quoad sacra* parishes added by the Church, the total number of separate charges in the Church of Scotland amounts to 1437. In addition to these there are 175 mission churches and stations, 25 of which will, within a very few years, be erected into parishes.

However detrimental to the best religious interests of the country the successive secessions may have been, they undoubtedly served to supply ordinances to the rapidly increasing population of the country. At the formation of the United Presbyterian Church in 1847, its congregations numbered some 500. It brought 600 into the larger union of 1900, while the Free Church brought 1106. Since that time the useful process of amalgamating small adjacent congregations has gone on; and the United Free Church has now 1610 churches and 27 mission and preaching stations.

Another distinguishing feature of the period points to a widening view of Christian responsibility. Largely under the inspiration of the Committee on Christian Life and Work founded in 1869 under the guidance of Professor Charteris, it has been recognized that the Church must touch the life of the individual at many points; and in order to discharge its duties both to its own members and to those who have drifted beyond its pale, many organizations have been formed. The training of the young, the helping of the destitute, and the uplifting of the submerged, as well as agencies for the mutual help of Church members, have enlisted great numbers of workers. Laymen and women (including those enrolled in the revived order of Deaconesses), are being used in the service of the Church as never before both at home and abroad. No Church is considered complete without its halls for this varied work. At the same time a new and finer spirit has manifested itself in the matter of church architecture and construction. Many ancient cathedrals, including St Giles's in Edinburgh, Iona, Dunkeld, Dunblane and Brechin; and other churches have been restored, and many new churches erected in a style worthy of their purpose.

That the Churches still maintain their hold on the people is evidenced by indisputable facts. In 1843, before the Disruption, the communicants of the Church of Scotland did not number more than 14 per cent. of the population. In 1908 they numbered nearly 15 per cent. and those of the United Free Church over 10 per cent.; taken together they amounted to 25 per cent. Their activities and their contributions have increased in a still greater proportion.

It only remains to say something of the movements in theology and worship which have lifted Scottish Presbyterianism out of the comparative stagnation of the preceding two centuries.

The Church of Scotland all through its history has possessed as a Church greater freedom than the Church of England or any other Church in close alliance with a State, but up to, and indeed after the middle of last century it would not be an exaggeration to say that its clergy possessed less freedom of thought or at least of expressing their thoughts, than either those of the Church of England or of many other Churches not connected with a State.

The saddest stain upon the annals of the Church in the nineteenth century was the deposition in 1831 of John Macleod Campbell of Row. Moderates and Evangelicals united to expel a man of great spiritual activity and devoted Christian character, for alleged heresy with regard to the Atonement.

The Westminster Confession of Faith has long held dominion over the minds of men in Scotland. It contains much more than a Creed in the ordinary acceptance of the term, and is indeed rather a manifesto of Christian belief and opinion as entertained by learned and pious men at the time it was compiled. It never claims infallibility for itself, but even disavows the claim in professing to derive all authority from the supreme standard of Holy Scripture, unto which, it says, "Nothing at any time is to be added whether by new revelations of the Spirit or traditions of men."

The formula by which a minister declared the Confession to be the confession of his own faith was meant, as we have seen (p. 109), to ensure the loyalty of Episcopal ministers entering the Church. It came to be considered as binding every minister to absolute conformity with every jot and tittle in the Confession. Against this conception protests began to be raised, and the name of Principal John Tulloch of St Andrews is deservedly remembered as a pioneer in the movement for greater freedom. Protesting against the rigid enforcement of the statements in the Confession, he said: "They are but the best thoughts about Christian truth, as those who framed them thought in their time. Intrinsically they are nothing more, and any claim of infallibility for them is the worst of all kinds of popery." This view came to be accepted by the Church, and finally a clause in the Scottish Churches Act of 1905 authorized it to frame its own formula. The formula framed by the General Assembly in 1910 runs thus: "I hereby subscribe the Confession of faith, declaring that I accept it as the Confession of this Church and that I believe the fundamental doctrines of the Christian Faith contained therein." This measure of liberty in matters of detail meets the actual conditions of mind prevalent in the Church. The United Free Church also has taken up a position of greater freedom with respect to the Confession.

Dr Norman Macleod of the Barony Church, Glasgow, was another leader in the movement for reasonable liberty of religious thought and practice. He encountered bitter opposition and even enmity from rigid Sabbatarians in his attempts to place the observance of the Lord's day upon New Testament rather than on Old Testament grounds. But eventually his views came to be very generally accepted.

The most famous heresy case, however, occurred in the Free Church. Professor Robertson Smith of the Aberdeen College, a man of brilliant genius and devout life, gave great offence by his publications on Old Testament literature, which set aside the traditional views of the authorship and were therefore held to undermine the inspiration of sundry books of Scripture; and in 1881 he was removed from his duties by the General Assembly. But opinion has moved rapidly since that time, and the latitude permitted on such questions is now as wide in the United Free Church as in the Church of Scotland.

In the conduct of public worship a vast change has been witnessed. The conviction that public prayers demand order and previous preparation, the study of ancient liturgies, and the desire to bring congregational devotions into harmony with the best usages in the universal Church, have wrought this change. Dr Robert Lee, of Old Greyfriars Church, Edinburgh, suffered much in his championship of this cause. His prayers, written and read, and the introduction by him of an organ were much opposed. But now musical instruments are generally used, "human" hymns as well as the Psalms may be heard in almost every Church, and prayers are more orderly and more dignified in language.

The size and scope of this volume have made it necessary to concentrate attention entirely upon the historical development of Presbyterianism in Scotland. It is not a history of the Church of Scotland. No attempt has been made to delineate the character of the protagonists in the many conflicts mentioned, or to throw dramatic incidents into relief. The peculiarly intimate relations which Presbyterianism has established in Scotland between the ministry and all the interests of the Church on the one hand, and the people and their interests on the other hand, have been left without illustration.

One remark, however, must be made.

However widely the Scotland of the twentieth century may differ from the Scotland of Knox and Melville, it cannot be denied that their principles, shorn of some rigour and brought into proportion by experience, rule the ecclesiastical life of Scotland to-day. The government is Presbyterian—orderly, simple, and capable of meeting every crisis by its inherent strength, its close touch with the people, and by its store of precedents accumulated during centuries of development. The happy combination of the clergy and the representatives of the laity in the same courts has kept the Church in constant sympathy with the mind and needs of the country. Presbyterianism has justified itself in Scotland by its adaptation to the religious needs of three centuries and a half.

The intolerant zeal of early days has, it is true, been replaced by a more charitable temper. Yet Scotland is as stedfastly Protestant as ever. That very education which Scottish Churchmen have done so much to give to the people has made it possible for these Churchmen to relax the vigilance of their anti-Romanism, and to sanction as lawful to Christian liberty what once might have been construed as concession to Romish error. The zeal of Knox and

Melville for education has never been wanting in the Church. Left at the Reformation with the merest pittance from its ancient patrimony to maintain its ministry, the Church and individual Churchmen, out of their poverty and with little countenance from the State, did much to establish schools for the people. Not till 1696 did Parliament come effectually to their aid. But from that time till 1872, when the Parish Schools of Scotland were handed over to form the basis of a national compulsory system of education, the alliance between Church and School in Scotland was perhaps the nation's greatest blessing. Even to-day, when the financial resources of the State make it the only organization able to cope with the demands of education, the Church exercises a constant and friendly influence upon the whole detail of instruction and administration. No ecclesiastical differences embitter educational affairs in Scotland.

Scotland's contribution to theological thought lies, of course, outside the scope of this work. Despite its meagre Church and College endowments, it has furnished names of renown in the exposition of Christian doctrine and the defence of the Christian faith. But, beyond doubt, the principal services of Scottish theological schools have been in the formation of a thoughtful and reverent people, accustomed to great themes and serious reflection upon them, by the ministrations of an educated clergy, whose first voca-

tion has always been held to be the preaching of the
Gospel in its fulness, and the elucidation of the mind
of the Spirit in the Word of God.

While all these things lie outside Presbyterianism
as a bare system of Church government, they have
been vitally connected with it in its Scottish development; and it may perhaps be contended with reason
that they are all results of a consistent conception of
the duties of the individual Christian and of the
Christian Church, which the Providence of God and
the fidelity of the Reformers in Scotland permitted
to be worked out with unusual completeness.

With the general trend in all the Churches towards
a more liberal theology, and the growing conscious-
ness of a common responsibility for the religious
advancement of Scotland and of the world, the feeling among the Presbyterian Churches of Scotland
has continually tended to grow more kindly. One
in ancient tradition, one in Church government, one
in their common use of the national Universities,
serving substantially the same classes of the community with the same form of worship, and in recent
years even with the same collection of hymns, being
also continually assimilated by cross-currents of
literary, social, political and religious thought, their
separate existence has moved the stranger to wonder.

Within the last few years the Church of Scotland
and the United Free Church have drawn more

closely together, and are seeking by conference to discover their common ground and to understand each other's distinctive principles. It is not beyond hope that a way may be found of combining the principles of National Religion and of Spiritual Independence. The Churches have narrowed down the area of what Scotland knows as "the fundamentals"; and the State also has learned to hold its hand. If in outward organization these Churches can attain the unity already felt in spirit, the Scottish Church, National, Free and Presbyterian, will have reached a more perfect condition as the spiritual organ of the nation than even the undivided Church of the Reformation, and may play a worthy part in the re-union of Christendom and the evangelization of the world.

BOOKS SUGGESTED FOR FURTHER STUDY

P and *E* added after the names of works indicate that they are written from the Presbyterian or the Episcopalian point of view respectively. No attempt is made at a complete bibliography, for which the bibliographical appendixes to the chapters dealing with Scotland in the *Cambridge Modern History* may be consulted.

i. *General History.*

Cunningham, J. The Church History of Scotland (*P*). 2 vols. Edinburgh, 1882.

Grub, G. An Ecclesiastical History of Scotland (*E*). 4 vols. Edinburgh, 1861.

Mathieson, W. L. Politics and Religion in Scotland. 2 vols. Glasgow, 1902.

Craik, Sir Henry. A Century of Scottish History. 2 vols. Edinburgh, 1901.

See also the standard histories of Scotland.

ii. *The Scottish Church at the rise of Presbyterianism.*

Dowden, Bishop J. The Medieval Church in Scotland. Glasgow, 1910.

Patrick, D. Statutes of the Scottish Church (Scottish History Society). Edinburgh, 1907.

iii. *The beginnings of Presbyterianism* (1560-1625).

Knox, John. Historie of the Reformation (edited by D. Laing and reprinted by Thin). Edinburgh, 1895.

—— The Book of the Universal Kirk (edited by Peterkin). Edinburgh, 1839, and other dates.

Spottiswoode, Archbishop. History of the Church of Scotland (Spottiswoode Society). Edinburgh, 1847–1851.

Calderwood, David. The True History of the Church of Scotland (Wodrow Society). Edinburgh, 1842–1849.

iv. *The later seventeenth century.*

Hewison, J. King. The Covenanters (*P*). 2 vols. Glasgow, 1908.

Story, R. H. William Carstares. London, 1874.

v. *The eighteenth century.*

Carlyle, Autobiography of Dr Alexander (of Inveresk: a Moderate), ed. J. Hill Burton. Edinburgh, 1860 (recently reprinted).

MacEwen, A. R. The Erskines (Evangelical). Edinburgh, 1900.

vi. *The nineteenth century.*

Hanna, W. Memoirs of Dr Thomas Chalmers. 4 vols. Edinburgh, 1849–1852.

Bryce, J. Ten Years of the Church of Scotland. 2 vols. Edinburgh, 1850.

Buchanan, R. The Ten Years' Conflict. 2 vols. Glasgow, 1849.

Charteris, A. H. Life of Professor James Robertson. Edinburgh, 1863.

See also many biographies of other eminent Church leaders.

vii. *Forms of worship.*

Sprott, G. W. The Worship and Offices of the Church of Scotland. Edinburgh, 1882.

McCrie, C. G. The Public Worship of Presbyterian Scotland. Edinburgh, 1892.

INDEX